MUAY THAI
UNLEASHED

Also by Erich Krauss

Beyond the Lion's Den (with Ken Shamrock)

Brawl

Jiu-Jitsu Unleashed (with Eddie Bravo)

Little Evil

On the Line

Wall of Flame

Warriors of the Ultimate Fighting Championships

Wave of Destruction

Guerrilla Jiu-Jitsu (with Dave Camarillo)

MUAY THAI
UNLEASHED

LEARN TECHNIQUE AND STRATEGY
FROM THAILAND'S WARRIOR ELITE

ERICH KRAUSS AND **GLEN CORDOZA**
WITH **TANA (CHUN) YINGWITAYAKHUN**

McGraw·Hill

New York   Chicago   San Francisco   Lisbon   London   Madrid   Mexico City
Milan   New Delhi   San Juan   Seoul   Singapore   Sydney   Toronto

The McGraw·Hill Companies

Library of Congress Cataloging-in-Publication Data

Krauss, Erich, 1971–.
    Muay Thai unleashed : learn technique and strategy from Thailand's warrior elite /
Erich Krauss and Glen Cordoza.
        p.   cm.
    Includes index.
    ISBN 0-07-146499-9 (alk. paper)
    1. Muay Thai—Thailand.   I. Cordoza, Glen.   II. Title.

GV1127.T45K73   2006
796.83095931—dc22   2006002287

1 2 3 4 5 6 7 8 9 0   DOC/DOC 0 9 8 7 6

ISBN-13: 978-0-07-146499-4
ISBN-10:   0-07-146499-9

Interior design by Think Design Group LLC

This book is for educational purposes. It is not intended as a substitute for individual fitness and health advice. Neither McGraw-Hill nor the authors shall have any responsibility for any adverse effects arising directly or indirectly as a result of information provided in this book.

McGraw-Hill books are available at special quantity discounts to use as premiums and sales promotions, or for use in corporate training programs. For more information, please write to the Director of Special Sales, Professional Publishing, McGraw-Hill, Two Penn Plaza, New York, NY 10121-2298. Or contact your local bookstore.

This book is printed on acid-free paper.

Contents

2 STANCE AND FOOTWORK 33

3 ATTACKS 53

4 DEFENSE AND COUNTERS

Basic Defense . . . .

Defensive Techniques . . . .

About This Book

Written by professional Muay Thai fighters and trainers, this book reveals the most commonly used techniques in Muay Thai competition through step-by-step photographs and easy to understand narrative. If you are interested in preparing mentally and physically for combat, acquiring training programs to make you a better fighter, incorporating practical moves into your current style, or simply understanding what it takes to be a practitioner of one of the most feared and dangerous martial arts, then step up to the counter and lay your money down. This book covers all the fundamentals of Muay Thai, including kicks, punches, elbow strikes, knee strikes, grappling (clinch), defense, counters, and an assortment of combinations. It shows you how to get the most out of training with focus mitts and Thai pads, as well as acquire drills to improve your conditioning and timing. As far as a comprehensive guide to Muay Thai techniques, no other book can compare. The book does not waste space with flashy moves that do not work—each technique has been tested time and again at the highest levels of competition. If you read and study this book from front to back, you will have an understanding of all the tools and techniques needed to compete on a professional level. Then it's just a matter of putting your newfound skills together, which the last chapters of this book will help you with.

This book will benefit those who wish to:

> Compete in Muay Thai
> Compete in mixed martial arts or kickboxing
> Learn a highly effective form of self-defense

MUAY THAI
UNLEASHED

INTRODUCTION TO MUAY THAI

The Evolution of Muay Thai

Thousands of years ago, Thai soldiers struggling to defend their land against invaders created a martial art that transformed their hands, legs, elbows, and knees into deadly weapons. Responsible for countless victories on hillsides and deep in the jungle, their system of fighting, now known as Muay Thai or the "science of eight limbs," was embraced by kings and the general populace from its inception. With the most competent warriors being hailed as heroes and adored by society, eventually the art was taken from the battlefield and adopted as a sport so young men with the determination and desire could experience a similar glory. Dirt fighting pits sprang up around the country, allowing practitioners to test their skills against one another. Wrapping their hands with hemp rope, and then sometimes dipping the rope in glue and then shards of glass, it was not uncommon for participants to fight to the death.

For hundreds of years Thai boxers laid everything on the line. It wasn't until the twentieth century that a more rigid set of rules was established to increase the longevity of the fighters. Cotton wraps and gloves replaced the hemp rope hand wraps, and the more vicious strikes such as head-butts and groin strikes were outlawed. Time limits and weight classes were also established. Although some die-hard fans and fighters felt such restrictions tainted the sport, the bouts only got more entertaining as fighters were allowed to hone their skills by avoiding serious injuries. Today, the sport harbors not only the best fighters in the world, but also some of the most impressive athletes.

Hundreds of training camps scattered throughout Thailand currently accept young athletes and transform them into world-class fighters. Unlike in most martial arts, practitioners are expected to fight on a monthly basis. The most technical and competent combatants compete in Rajadamnern, Lumpinee, and Channel 7 stadiums in Bangkok, and millions watch their aggressive, highly technical matches each week on television. And with competitors constantly refining and adding new techniques to their game, such as punches from Western boxing, practically every match guarantees a plethora of signature moves and nonstop action.

While for years the heart and dedication of Thai boxers and the ferocity of their fighting system was known by only a handful of foreigners, the advances in video technology and the country's booming tourist industry have introduced·the sport of Muay Thai to the world. Now thousands of foreigners travel each year to Thailand to live in a traditional camp, acquire the techniques of champions, and then return home to share their newfound skills. They have passed Thai boxing training regimens on to kickboxers and mixed martial arts (MMA) competitors, and in world-renowned fighting competitions such as K-1, PRIDE, and the Ultimate Fighting Championship (UFC), the strikes and stratagems of Muay Thai can now be found in nearly every bout. Although such skills can be acquired in a gym in nearly every major city in the world, the choice place to learn Muay Thai is still its birthplace, where techniques haven't been watered down or altered and the average native one-hundred-forty-pound fighter can push the top foreign heavyweight to his limits.

A Day in the Life of a Thai Boxer

There is no clock on the wall, but you know it's time to wake up because underneath the small wood shack in which you sleep two stray dogs are fighting, and off in the distance roosters are booming their early morning wake-up call. Sitting up on the cement floor, you look around. Some of the other boys, all between twelve and eighteen years of age, are already breaking down their mosquito nets.

It's four o'clock, and back in your hill tribe your mother, father, and siblings are still asleep, getting their rest for a hard day of labor. It's been over a year since you have seen them, and you long for the smells of home and the hours running free through the jungle. Life back there was kind, but with no money for your education, your options were few. Your parents knew your life would get progressively harder as the years went by, and they made the difficult choice to send you away. The twelve boys with whom you share this hut are your family now. You go to them when sad or in need of advice. You take care of them, and they take care of you. It is warming to see that most of them have smiles on their faces at this early morning hour.

You follow the crowd out into the darkness. The trainers are off somewhere, but for the first part of the morning you need no instruction or supervision. All of you know exactly what is expected, so you begin to run. Across the cement platform that holds two rings and a dozen heavy bags, down a winding trail through the jungle, and out onto the road. Your legs are sluggish from the day before and your lungs feel tight, but all the motivation you need is the boy directly ahead. You match his strides, and eventually your legs warm and your lungs loosen. After an hour meandering through the mountains, enjoying the wildlife that will take to hiding as the sun comes up, you finally return to camp and your ten-kilometer warm-up run is out of the way.

Hunger pains set in, but you push them aside. You follow your twelve brothers into the ring and begin shadowboxing, throwing jabs, uppercuts, elbows, kicks, and knees into the open air. You visualize an opponent, but instead of throwing knockout blows, you dance around him, focusing on grace and timing and fluidity. For fifteen minutes you become a butterfly, and then you climb out of the ring and take position in front of one of the heavy bags dangling from a steel pole. Rain comes suddenly and pounds down on the straw roof, filling the open-air gym with freshness. Your body is warm and your mind alert, and with the chime of a bell you tear into the old, chafed leather of the bag with punches and kicks. The bag is your adversary for the moment, and every punch has the capability to shatter your opponent's jaw. Every kick has the capability to crack ribs.

For fifteen minutes straight you unleash. There can be no laziness, no half efforts. The instructors have turned up, and each is armed with a whomping-stick, an instrument they are not timid to use.

The bell chimes again, and you take a step closer to the bag. Two years ago, when your parents first sent you here at the age of twelve, your body fought against your mind at this stage of training. After the run and the rounds, it seemed impossible to go on. But now your muscles are stronger, your bones harder, and, most important, your mind unrelenting. You wrap your arms around the bag as if it were an opponent's neck and shift from punches and kicks to knees. You drive your left knee into the solar plexus of the bag, and then the right. You do this over and over with no end in sight. After three hundred repetitions, an instructor tells you to stop. You take a step back, but there is no time to catch your breath. You lift your front leg and drive the ball of your foot into the bag. A hundred push kicks with your right leg and then a hundred with your left. With that out of the way you drop down, welcoming the cold cement on your back. You blast out the two hundred sit-ups in a matter of minutes because if you're slow the other boys will beat you to the shower outside the temple. The last to the showers is the last to the breakfast table, and the last at the breakfast table rarely gets enough food to feed his belly.

As you join the crowd around a mat on the floor after your shower, two of the younger boys arrive with food from the market. When you first arrived to the camp, it was your job to fetch the food and clean up afterward. But you have moved up the chain, and now only five boys are above you on the hierarchy. You pay respect to the more experienced of your peers and allow them to help themselves first, just as the younger boys pay a similar respect to you. When you get your helping of soup, you gulp it down because seconds are up for grabs. This day you are too slow and will have to make do with your hunger until supper. You hand your bowl to a kid of twelve years and thank him kindly as he hurries off to the washbasin.

There is no chitchat after breakfast because everyone is rushing back to the hut to put on their school uniform. As always, everyone is late. The three-mile walk to school quickly turns into a run, and your body doesn't get a rest until you finally slide into a chair in front of the teacher and turn your mind to something other than fighting. For the next six hours, you try to learn what nearly every other child in class has all evening to study. Many of your fellow students come from richer homes, and although a few of them can be considered acquaintances, none of them have ever invited you over to play. Under the bright lights of an arena you are admired by hundreds, but in the classroom you are known to be poor and considered lower-class by those with money. It bothers you at times, but in your heart you know you're special. You send the money from your fights home to your parents, allowing them to buy necessities they never before had. Maybe some of the money will help put your younger brother through school when the time comes. And besides, living in a room with twelve other boys, you are never alone.

It is pouring rain on the walk home from school, and you're hunched over your book bag, trying to keep your homework dry. When you finally step into the hut, you set down your bag and stare at your sleeping mat for a long while. You have time for a fifteen-minute nap, but you come to the conclusion that it will only make you more tired than you already are. A few of the other boys are wrestling in a corner, and you opt to join in. Laughter circles around, but it comes to a halt just as quickly as it began. It is time for afternoon training.

The rain is coming down harder now, but despite the distraction, the five-kilometer run comes much easier than the run you did that morning. You conclude your warm-up back in the gym by skipping rope for half an hour. With your body warm and relaxed, you do another twenty-five minutes of shadowboxing and another twenty-five minutes relentlessly attacking the heavy bag. The true hell is yet to come, but every strike on the bag is a knockout blow, because the instructors are circling with their whomping-sticks. They don't put down their sticks until everyone is finished on the bags, and they only put them down because their hands and skills are required. Onto their arms they strap heavy Thai pads, and the nearest instructor calls you into the ring. This middle-aged man has been around you eight hours a day for the past two years. He knows your weaknesses and strengths, and he knows just what it takes to get the most out of your mind and body.

He holds up the pads at shoulder level on his left side, and instantly you throw a right Thai kick. The pads quickly shoot over to his right side, and you throw a left Thai kick. Then the pads are down low, positioned in front of his belly, and you dig in with a rear knee. You throw ten, twenty, fifty strikes before the round is over. You get a minute to rest, and then it's back at it, launching a series of combinations into the pads and toughening the bones in your shins and knuckles in the process. After you do five three-minute rounds, the instructor takes a step back and calls over one of your peers. The two of you wrap your arms around each other in the center of the ring and begin fighting for the most dominant clinch position. The boy in front of you is your friend, a brother, but for the moment he is your opponent. You work your technique and timing, trying to throw him to the ground or open him up so you can land a knee to his ribs or an elbow to his jaw. After ten minutes of nonstop grappling, you break and another boy steps forward. You go through the same exhausting battle for another ten minutes. By the time you step out of the ring, an hour and a half has passed. Your lungs are on fire, and your neck feels like jelly from all the pushing and pulling. You want to go to the hut and lie down, but the instructors have picked their whomping-sticks back up.

It's back to the heavy bags to do another four hundred straight knees and another hundred Thai kicks. You get a few whomps from a stick because your legs are wobbly and your arms are too heavy to hold up to protect your face. You eventually reach your quota and then drop down for push-ups, sit-ups, and a host of other strength-building exercises. By the time you make it to the cooldown and stretch, your body has nothing left. You want nothing more than to go to the hut and lie down, but several of the boys have gotten injured during training, and you go to them to rub tiger balm on their joints and offer emotional support. You help carry them over to the showers and then the dinner table. You will pamper them in the days to come because they have done the same for you. The majority of you will be stepping into the ring this weekend, just as you did the weekend past, and all of your survival depends upon your ability to fight. And what allows you to fight, to keep up this grueling regimen day after day, year after year, is the support of one another.

After supper, you return to the hut and find a place to spread out your mat and hang up your mosquito net. Your body and mind are exhausted, and tomorrow you have to do it all over again. You fall asleep dreaming of one day becoming a champion of your province, and then getting picked up by a gym in Bangkok and fighting under the bright lights of Rajadamnern or Lumpinee stadiums. The likelihood of one of you making it that far is slim, yet you never give up hope. Becoming a champion is your one chance to escape poverty. It is your chance to achieve greatness.

Training Gear

There are still a few Muay Thai training camps that can't afford protective gear to ensure the safety of their fighters or modern equipment to enhance training. They have little more than the environment around them, and they make use of it, kicking banana trees, punching dangling coconuts, and fighting barefist with one another. Although this method of training has produced some exceptional fighters over the centuries, there is no reason for someone who has a little bit of money to ignore the advancements in training gear. The majority of Thai boxing camps now utilize gloves, shin guards, kicking pads, and a host of bags to get the most out of their fighters and to keep them injury-free for their upcoming bouts. With the popularity of Muay Thai soaring around the world, dozens of companies are producing quality equipment that can endure the rigors of a Thai boxing regimen at an affordable price. However, you must be careful of what you purchase. While some equipment is well made and will be beneficial to your training, much of it is shoddy and will only slow you down. The essential gear to get started is listed below.

HAND WRAPS

Hand wraps are a must when training in Muay Thai. Most of the bags and pads you will be hitting during training are hard and not very forgiving. If your hands aren't wrapped, all it will take is one wrong punch to injure your knuckles or wrist. It is also just as important to wrap your hands when fighting or sparring in the gym. Crashing your fist into an opponent's face can be the same as punching a wall, and few fighters can punch a wall with full force and not injure their hand. When sparring, wrapping your hands should suffice because your goal is not to knock your opponent out, but rather practice and hone your techniques. However, when you step into the ring, your goal is to do as much damage to your opponent as possible, and this means striking with bad intentions. Most fighters pack layers of tape over their hand wraps before competition to create a cast-mold for added protection. This is a detailed science and should be done by an experienced trainer.

While in the past Thai boxers used hemp rope to protect the fragile bones in their hands, more practical hand wraps can be purchased at almost any athletic store. Deciding which type to buy largely depends upon your personal preference. Nearly all wraps are made from cotton or elastic and range from five to fifteen feet in length. If you plan on doing some heavy hitting, then you will be better off purchasing the longer wraps. They won't be as easy to put on, but they will provide better protection. The most popular brands are Twins, Fairtex, and

Windy. Price will depend upon where you purchase them, but they shouldn't cost more than ten dollars.

Once you have the wraps there are several different ways to put them on, depending on how complete a wrap you want and what style of wraps you're using. When first starting out, you should have an instructor take you through it step-by-step until you can do it on your own. Wrapping your hands isn't as easy as it sounds, and when doing it unsupervised for the first time you're likely to wrap them too loose or too tight. Your goal is to make sure the wrap covers all areas of your hand, providing the main protection to your knuckles, wrist, and thumb. If you've wrapped your hands correctly, you should be able to make a tight fist without any discomfort, yet also have the wrap tight enough that it doesn't come loose during training. Listed below are two methods of wrapping, but if you get confused or find the wraps uncomfortable, consult an instructor.

Basic Hand Wrap (Minimal Protection)

1. Place the small loop at the end of the wrap around your thumb.
2. Run the wrap across the top of your wrist, then loop it around your wrist several times.
3. From your wrist, run the wrap across the top of your hand to your knuckles. Loop the wrap across and around your knuckles four times.
4. From your knuckles, run the wrap down across the top of your hand to your wrist, then loop the wrap around your wrist four times.
5. From your wrist, run the wrap up and across the top of your hand to your knuckles. Loop the wrap around your knuckles two more times.
6. From your knuckles, run the wrap across your palm to your thumb. Loop the wrap completely around your thumb so that it ends up back at your wrist.
7. Loop the remainder of the wrap around your wrist. If you have a lot of wrap left over, you can go back over your knuckles. However, the end of the wrap should wind up back at your wrist. If your wraps have Velcro, secure it tightly. If your wraps do not have Velcro, tuck the end under the existing loops at the wrist.

Advanced Hand Wrap

1. To wrap your right hand, place the loop at the end of the wrap against the knuckle of your right index finger. Holding it in place with your right thumb, use your left hand to loosely loop the wrap around your knuckles four times.

2. Slide the wrap down your fingers and place the bundle on top of your knuckles. To hold it in place, pinch the bundle between your right thumb and index finger.

3. To secure the protective bundle on top of your knuckles, loop the wrap around your knuckles several times. You should now be able to release your thumb without the bundle slipping up or down your hand.

4. From your knuckles, run the wrap down across the top of your hand and under your thumb. From here, loop the wrap around your thumb.

5. Once you've made the loop around your thumb, run the wrap over the top of your wrist, and then loop it around your wrist several times.

6. From the inside of your wrist, run the wrap over the top of your hand and through the gap between your index finger and middle finger. Loop the wrap around your knuckles to hold it in place.

7. From your knuckles, run the wrap down across the top of your hand and loop it around your wrist.

8. From the inside of your wrist, run the wrap up the top of your hand and through the gap between your middle finger and ring finger. Loop the wrap around your knuckles to hold it in place.

9. From your knuckles, run the wrap down across the top of your hand and loop it around your wrist.

10. From the inside of your wrist, run the wrap up the top of your hand and through the gap between your ring finger and pinky. Loop it around your knuckles to hold the wrap in place.

11. From your knuckles, run the wrap down the top of your hand and loop around your wrist. If you have an extra foot of wrap, you can loop it around your thumb for added protection. To keep the wrap in place, secure the Velcro strap or tuck the end of the wrap under the material guarding your wrist.

GLOVES

Gloves are another piece of protective equipment that should always be used when sparring, doing bag work, or hitting anything in the gym. There are a few different styles of gloves you can utilize when training. Basic bag gloves are generally very small, usually about five ounces. They can be used for light bag work and are recommended for clinch sparring so you don't use your fingers to grab or accidentally stick a finger in your opponent's eye. Most have a thumb enclosure and an elastic tie around the wrist, making them easy to slip on and off.

When doing heavy bag work or padded rounds with an instructor, you generally want to use eight- to ten-ounce gloves that have a thumb enclosure and a Velcro strap around the wrist. For sparring, fourteen- to sixteen-ounce gloves are preferred for safety. Lace-up gloves provide better wrist support and last longer than the ones with a Velcro strap because the Velcro tends to lose its stick over time, but they can take longer to pull on and off, resulting in an interruption in your training.

When searching for gloves, make sure they are made entirely or mostly of leather and that they have latex foam or something comparable for padding. If you don't want to spend a heap of money buying an assortment of gloves, simply buy fourteen-ounce gloves and use them for everything. It's always good to try them on before laying your money down, but if you're ordering them through a catalog or over the Internet, pay attention to whether they are marked small, medium, or large, and choose the one that will best fit your hand. Generally, the heavier the gloves the bigger they will be. If you're training at a gym, there will probably be an assortment of gloves for the students to wear. It's recommended that you try out as many brands and weights as possible to see what fits you best. However, gym gloves tend to be smelly and molded to someone else's hand. Buying your own pair is seldom a bad investment. The most popular brands on the market are Fairtex, Twins, and Windy.

CUP

A cup is an essential piece of equipment that you'll not regret having if the unfortunate kick or knee finds its way to your groin. The groin protectors in ancient times were made from tree bark or seashells and fastened in place with rope, but thankfully they have come a long way due to advancements in technology. Nowadays you can buy many different types of cups, most of which are made from plastic or steel. The plastic ones are generally suitable only for training and light sparring because a solid kick or knee can easily shatter them, causing much more pain than if you weren't wearing a cup at all. The ones made from steel are highly recommended for hard sparring, and in Thailand they are mandatory for competition. If you find wearing a steel cup during training or sparring uncomfortable, the next best option is to wear a belly protector that covers your lower abdomen as well as your groin. Belly protectors are constructed from latex foam and provide you with adequate protection against light strikes.

Before purchasing a groin protector, you should always make sure it fits. Most are one-size-fits-all and accommodate the average-sized groin. You can also buy special fitted cups that range from small to extra large. You know where you stand, so don't fool yourself. A perfect fit is key.

SHIN PADS

Shin pads are used for sparring, contact training, and to protect a banged-up shin while kicking the heavy bag or Thai pads. There are numerous different styles of shin pads on the market. Some shin pads cover only the shin, while others cover the shin and foot. Some have Velcro straps, while others have lace-up straps. There are also soft cotton shin pads, but they are usually worn underneath the leather shin pads for added protection. If you are planning on doing hard fight training, the best ones to purchase are the leather shin pads with latex foam encasing that protect both your shin and foot. The ones with Velcro straps are the easiest to take on and off, but the ones with lace-up straps tend to last longer. It's all a matter of preference. When you find a pair of shin pads that you like, the most important thing is to make sure they fit. The top of the pad should come up to your knee and cover both sides of your shin. A good pair will cost between forty and one hundred dollars.

MOUTHPIECE

You will need to purchase a mouthpiece before you begin Muay Thai training. It should be worn for all contact training, but it's also a good idea to wear it while kicking the bags or pads. This will help you get accustomed to breathing with it in and having a bulky piece of plastic in your mouth. There are shapes and sizes on the market to fit everyone, even people with braces. You can choose a single-layer mouthpiece, which clings to your upper teeth, or a dual-layer mouthpiece, which fits your upper and lower teeth and locks your jaw in place. Those who choose the single layer usually do so because this type makes it easier to breathe and tends to be more comfortable. Those who choose the dual fit usually do so for overall protection (upon impact, the dual design prevents the lower jaw from smashing into the base of the skull, thereby helping prevent knockouts).

There are many quality brands of mouthpieces on the market: Shock Doctor, Brain-Pad, Wipps. The single-layer mouthpiece will cost between five and twenty dollars, while a dual-layer mouthpiece will cost anywhere from twenty to forty dollars. You can also have one specially made to fit your teeth by your dentist, which will obviously cost a lot more. This isn't as necessary today due to the quality of mouthpieces available, all of which can be molded to fit your teeth using the boil and bite method:

1. Bring a pot of water to a light boil.
2. Dip your mouthpiece into the water until it turns soft—this usually won't take more than fifteen seconds.

3. Remove mouthpiece and give it a few seconds to cool.
4. Place it in your mouth and bite down for a few seconds, sucking in gently.
5. Remove the mouthpiece and let it cool.

HEADGEAR

It is important to set terms before sparring with someone in the gym. If you and your training partner agree to go light, head-gear usually isn't necessary. If both of you want to go hard, then wearing headgear is highly recommended. Strapping protective gear onto your head doesn't mean you aren't tough; it just means that you want to prevent injury so you can keep training. It is also recommended that you wear headgear when sparring someone for the first time because you don't know his skill level or if he will suddenly pick up the pace when he gets hit.

There are many brands and styles of headgear you can choose from. Muay Thai camps will usually have open-face headgear or headgear with a padded face bar to protect the nose. Both are good, but having the face bar is recommended because it doesn't hurt anything and it will help prevent a broken nose. One thing to keep in mind while shopping for this piece of equipment is the durability and quality of the material—a leather outer shell with a suede leather interior tends to be the most comfortable and durable. The ones that lace up tend to last longer than the ones with Velcro straps. Most are one-size-fits-all. The open-face headgear will usually cost between twenty and sixty dollars, while the full-face protection will cost between sixty and one hundred dollars.

JUMP ROPE

Skipping rope is a great way to develop rhythm, cardio conditioning, and strength in the legs, as well as coordinate your upper body with your lower body. Muay Thai jump ropes are a bit different than those used in other gyms. Most Western boxers use the speed ropes made from rubber or rope. They are small, light, and thin. Muay Thai ropes are thicker and a lot heavier than the speed ropes. They are usually made of thick plastic or rubber rope and have wooden handles. The added thickness and weight are better for building strength and developing cardio conditioning. One thing to keep in mind, however, is these ropes are a lot less forgiving. At one time or another you are bound to get out of rhythm and whack the rope on your toes. This can cause even the toughest fighter to wince in pain. If you are totally new to rope jumping, it might be beneficial to acquire your technique and rhythm with a smaller rope first.

SPARRING VEST

Sparring vests are used in amateur Muay Thai competition and when doing full-contact sparring in the gym. They're designed to protect your midsection as well as give you a full range of motion. Most venues that host amateur competitions will provide you with all the needed gear before you enter the ring. However, if you are interested in buying your own sparring vest, look for products with leather or synthetic leather shells and foam chest plates. They will be the lightest and offer the most protection against full-power attacks. For design, you generally want a sparring vest that has an adjustable backing. The better brands will cost between eighty and one hundred dollars.

Coach's Equipment

THAI PADS

At least several pairs of Thai pads can be found in every legitimate Thai boxing training facility. Instructors use the pads to help students develop a sense of distance, timing, and accuracy, as well as to teach combinations. If there is not a Thai gym in your area and you plan on training at home with friends, it is highly recommended that you purchase a pair of Thai pads. But before you start training with them, it is important that you know how to correctly hold the pads to prevent injury to either the pad holder or the person doing the striking (see Chapter 5). What brand to buy depends a great deal on preference, but there are several things you must look for, the most important being that the pad is large enough to absorb the impact of a hard kick. Both the standard Thai pad, which measures sixteen inches tall, eight inches wide, and four inches thick, and the extended pad, which measures around seventeen inches tall, nine inches wide, and four inches thick, will usually suit just fine. Stay away from the ones with vinyl shells or synthetic leather shells because they will not last. All leather is a must. If you stick with the Windy, Twins, and Fairtex brands, you'll do fine. The ones with Velcro straps tend not to last as long as the ones with buckle straps, but they are easier and quicker to take on and off. A good pair of Thai pads will cost between $80 and $120.

FOCUS MITTS

Instructors use focus mitts to help their students practice punches and elbow strikes. Some coaches will also use them to help small children practice their kicks. When held right, they allow the student to develop a sense of distance, timing, and accuracy, as well as to work on different punching combinations. There are two different styles of focus mitts to choose from. The first is the standard mitt with a flat surface, which is good for straight punches and elbow combinations. The second mitt has a curved surface, and it is best suited for hooks and uppercut combinations due to its concave surface. It also takes some of the impact stress off the pad holder's joints. Both mitts are practical for Muay Thai training, and which style fills a gym depends upon the instructor's preference. For size, you'll want to make sure that they're at least an inch to an inch and a half thick and have a leather surface. With the Twins, Fairtex, and Windy brands, this is usually the case. The ones with buckle straps are difficult to take on and off, but they tend to last a long time. The ones with Velcro straps are easy to take on and off, but they generally wear out more quickly. The prices vary, but you should be able to get good quality focus mitts for sixty to eighty dollars.

COACH'S SPARRING GLOVES

Coach's sparring gloves are focus mitts and boxing gloves rolled into one. They should have a flat area on the palm that the student can strike, usually with a white dot to help with accuracy, as well as a padded glove that the instructor can use to strike at the student and keep him moving. These gloves are especially good for working on counteroffensive techniques. A good pair will cost between eighty and one hundred dollars.

KICKING SHIELD

The kicking shield is another piece of equipment you can find in most Muay Thai training facilities. It's great for practicing low kicks, which are difficult to perform using the Thai pads. It's also a wonderful piece of equipment for absorbing full power knees from all ranges of combat. There are two different styles. One is curved, and the other is flat. The curved one can accommodate a wider range of techniques, while the flat one is best suited for straight-on attacks such as knees and push kicks. The shells made entirely from leather will last ten times as long as the ones made from synthetic leather, but they are not as forgiving. A high-quality kicking shield will cost between $90 and $120.

BELLY PAD

Thai pads and focus mitts allow an instructor to teach offensive techniques such as hard Thai kicks and punches. The belly pad protects an instructor's stomach, chest, and ribs and allows him to teach defensive techniques such as push kicks and knees. The best ones have a leather shell, oval-shaped padding that protects the entire midsection, and an adjustable buckle closure. A high-quality belly pad will range between fifty and eighty dollars.

HEAVY BAG

When you're not getting personal attention from an instructor or sparring with your fellow students, much of your training will be done on a heavy bag. You can use it to develop power by unleashing with your punches, kicks, elbows, and knees. You can use it to develop timing and a sense of distance by moving around the bag and striking it as it swings toward you. You can use it to develop endurance by throwing hundreds of kicks or punches or knees in succession. You can use it to practice clinch techniques by wrapping your hands around the top of the bag as if it were an opponent's head. Purchasing a heavy bag will be one of the best investments you can make for your Muay Thai training, and there are several things you should consider before buying one. First, you do not want to buy a cheap bag because it will only fall apart after a couple days of hard training. Cheap bags are easy to spot because they are made from anything other than leather or thick canvas. Second, you do not want to buy a bag that will only be suited for throwing punches. If you are going to invest in a bag, you might as well spend a few extra bucks and get a long bag that drops all the way down to the floor. This will allow you to throw low kicks as well as upper body techniques.

Once you purchase a bag, there are many things to fill it with, but a combination of sand and cloth usually works best. It will be hard and heavy and not very forgiving, but that is what you want because it will prepare you for the reality of striking an opponent, who will also be hard and heavy and not very forgiving. However, you should be aware that the bottom of the bag is going be a lot harder than the top because the sand is more heavily packed. If your shins are not conditioned, you should spend a few weeks or months callusing your shins by throwing rib kicks before you attempt any hard low kicks.

There are several other bags that will help your training, but they are not nearly as important as the heavy bag. If you have some money left over after purchasing all of your mandatory gear, then a speed bag, top and bottom bag, and punching dummy are good investments. It is also nice to have a boxing ring in which to spar and do your pad work. Training in a ring will get you accustomed to the canvas floor and the limited space in which you have to work. It will also teach you how the ropes can be used to both your advantage and disadvantage. But with most rings costing several thousand dollars, they are a luxury few can afford.

Competition Versus Exercise

Not everyone who learns Muay Thai has the intention of one day stepping into the ring to compete. Training in Thai boxing can be an excellent way to get into shape, have fun, and learn a realistic form of self-defense. It is argued by many, however, that the only way to truly learn Muay Thai is to fight in competition. In Thailand, most gyms will accept only those who agree to fight. This rule is not strictly enforced with the thousands of foreigners who come to train at the camps every year, but it is highly recommended. Fighting is by far the best way to know if the techniques you are learning actually work. If such a path is one you desire, it is important that you acquire a different mind-set than those who are training for recreation. You must put forth a 110 percent effort every time you step into the gym, which should be twice a day, six days a week. The only person who will suffer from heading into battle unprepared is yourself, and perhaps the reputation of your gym.

Levels of Learning

If you're just starting out in Muay Thai, don't get discouraged if you're not picking up the techniques as quickly as those around you. It is a fact of life that some are just more naturally talented than others. Muay Thai involves so many different aspects, and just being naturally talented doesn't make someone a good Muay Thai fighter. Many people's strengths, such as impeccable timing and inherent fighting strategy, aren't recognized until much later in the game. The important thing is not to move too fast or try to grasp everything within the first few days of training. It is a very complex art that takes a lifetime of hard work to master.

Preparing for a Fight

In order to prepare for a fight you must achieve a warrior's mind-set, and this can be accomplished by simply training hard. How hard? Well, you have to train harder than your opponent, and since you often don't know who your opponent is or what he's doing in his gym, you have to assume that he is training all the time. This should force you to put in as many hours as possible. Maintaining such an intense schedule can certainly take the fun out of the sport, which is the reason you should pick and choose your fights—especially if you're not planning on fighting for a career. Most Thai boxers in Thailand fight every two to three weeks, and year-round they maintain a demanding training regimen. Their lifestyle is one many of us find hard to envision. Unless you've been raised on Thai boxing or have superhuman mental and physical stamina, the chances are you will find it very difficult to adopt and sustain their way of life. The important part is that you maintain the intense workouts for the fights that you do choose. The last thing you want is to wonder if you've put enough time into training while climbing over the ropes, because it can lead to increased stress and early fatigue. A confident fighter is a good fighter and almost always the victor. He knows that he's prepared to the best of his ability, leaving no doubt in his mind that he can handle the challenge to come. He does not fear the coming pain because he has put himself through more pain in training than he could ever feel in the ring. He knows what it is like to be tired and fatigued, and he knows how to motivate himself for that extra push. Oftentimes, that extra push is what wins the fight.

Great in Training, Bad in the Ring

In your first couple of fights you will most likely use only half of what you really know. And when fighting, you will look about half as good as you do when hitting the pads or heavy bag. If you find this to be true like many fighters, don't get discouraged. With time and experience, this gap will gradually fade as you turn techniques into reactions. Just like the top fighters in Bangkok, you will learn how to clear your mind before battle and let instinct take over.

Showing Weakness

A fighter should never show any signs of weakness. When you're tired or something hurts, hide it. Letting your opponent know what is wrong with you will only make matters worse because he can then capitalize on your injury or use your suffering to fuel his confidence (remember, a confident fighter is a dangerous one). If you are tired and you give this away with facial expressions or by hanging out your tongue, your opponent will most likely pick up the pace in hopes of quickly ending the fight. If you show that your legs or ribs hurt, your opponent will most likely execute techniques that will open those areas up for an attack. No matter how bad you feel, nothing positive can come from giving it away. It is also important not to get discouraged by your opponent's actions. Sometimes a fighter will laugh or get cocky with his movements or facial expressions in an attempt to throw you off. Don't let this faze you or interrupt your concentration. When your opponent laughs at you after you land something clean, it usually means that your strike did some damage and he is trying to show both you and the judges that it didn't hurt. If this happens, a good strategy is to land that blow again and again until your opponent isn't smiling anymore.

Training Injured

Injuries are an unfortunate but inevitable occurrence in the fight game. At some point during training you're bound to run into a strained or pulled muscle, a dinger on your shin, a sprained ankle, a broken bone, extreme soreness, or a flare-up of an old injury. The most important thing when it comes to injuries is to listen to your body. If something hurts, don't do it. And do everything needed to treat that injury so that it heals properly. Most Thai boxers suffer from ankle problems, broken hands, and shin injuries due to the constant abuse to their bodies. Most also continue to train even though they are injured. However, they train in such a way that it doesn't aggravate their injuries. If you have a sore right shin, focus on knees and left kicks. If your hands are banged up, focus on lower body attacks. A good fighter is one who can adapt to any situation, and training when injured is one of them. Don't let a little injury take you out of training, especially if you have a fight coming up. The only reason to step out of training is if you have a spinal injury or something equally serious. If that is the case, do whatever you can to ensure that it heals properly, or you may never train again.

Winning Versus Losing

Whether you are competing in the gym or in a professional bout, there will be a sense of winning and losing. It is important to keep in mind that everybody at one point or another is going to lose. Don't let a loss get you down. Most professional Thai boxers are around the same skill level, and anything can happen during the course of the bout. In Thailand, it is not uncommon for two fighters to face each other half a dozen times, earning three victories apiece. However, you should never go into a bout thinking you are going to lose. Fighting is a tough sport, and if you doubt your ability to perform and win you should consider something else. If you are a competitive person by nature and happen to lose, don't let it break your spirit. Oftentimes you can learn more from a loss than you can from a win. You learn the areas in which you have to improve, and then you can take that knowledge back to the gym and polish out your weaknesses. Instead of making you feel like giving up, a loss should inspire you to be better than the competitor who beat you.

Respect

As in all martial arts, respect is key when training in Muay Thai. You should respect and honor your teacher, opponents, training partners, and community. Basically, represent Muay Thai in a positive manner. A true warrior's skill lies in how to avoid confrontation. Most Thai boxers are kind and caring people, and you would never know that they are stone-cold killers when pushed. If you are looking for respect, a nonconfrontational mind-set is the best way to earn it.

Finding the Right Gym in Thailand

The ability for foreigners to come to Thailand and learn the art of Muay Thai has improved phenomenally over the past few years. Having realized there is money to be made by opening their doors to tourists, dozens of Thai boxing training camps now openly invite men and women from around the world into their facilities.

Bangkok is the most expensive, but it has the best training facilities in Thailand. It's where all the top fighters end up at the peak of their careers, and as a result it boasts some of the best trainers, many of whom speak English. The most popular gyms cost about twenty-five to thirty dollars a day, depending upon what gym you're at, how long you plan to stay, and whether or not you plan to fight. With the trainers claiming half of your purse from a fight, you may not have to pay at all if you agree to fight on a weekly basis. If your reason for heading to Thailand is exclusively to train and you have money saved up, then Bangkok is the way to go. Not only will you be trained by the best, but you will also be training with the best.

Southern Thailand is probably the second most expensive place to train because of the beaches and the popular tourist attractions. The gyms are nice, and most have at least one trainer who can speak English. Northern Thailand also boasts excellent gyms, especially in the Chaing Mai area, and it will be a much cheaper route. Training will cost between two and five dollars a day, and the cost of living is just as cheap. There are a lot of competitions held throughout the year in this area, and you can usually land some good, fair fights.

Isaan and northeastern Thailand are where most of the top champions hail from, but the majority of gyms in this area are generally not well suited for tourism. If you have little money and are easily distracted from training, this might be the place for you. You can live on dollars a week, and there are few distractions in the area to pull you away from training. However, when taking up residence at a traditional camp not accustomed to training foreigners, you will be expected to train and live like the native fighters.

Whatever gym you choose to walk into, don't be shy—ask plenty of questions. Foreigners own many of the popular Thai boxing gyms, making it easy to discuss price and so forth. It's also usually not a good idea to tell them that you want to fight on your first day. It's better to give the gym a couple of trial days to make sure that the training is up to par and you're getting your money's worth. Take a look at the quality of instruction, and ask the other foreigners what they think of the place. Be sure that the trainers really care about whether or not you're learning the techniques properly. If they are just holding the pads for you, not constantly correcting your form, then you should leave and find another gym because the quality of training will only go down the longer you have been there.

Another thing to look out for is if the trainers immediately try to get you to fight. It can be a boost to your confidence, but in many cases the trainers are only after half of your purse, which they claim even if your opponent destroys you. A good gym won't throw you in the ring right away, and they won't pit you against someone who can easily defeat you. Before you do step into the ring, go to the fights of some of the other foreigners training at the gym and see if they are evenly matched bouts. If they are not, find another gym that can better gauge skill level.

Even when you find a gym you like, don't be afraid to venture out and experiment with other gyms. Most instructors won't mind as long as you tell them ahead of time. With every gym having a different training regimen, you can only benefit from diversifying. Once you find a gym that fits your needs, it will make traveling all that way pay off. A good gym will take care of you in and out of the ring. The instructors will treat you as family and make the whole experience worthwhile. You will walk away with a new group of loyal friends, world-class training, and perhaps a few fights under your belt. The key is not to give up until you find what you are looking for because it can be found.

Gym Etiquette in Thailand

Training camps in Thailand have special rules that all fighters must abide by, foreigners included. Thai people are generally kindhearted and understanding, and it's not in their nature to get upset if your actions go against their practiced etiquette. Nevertheless, you should make it a point to learn their rules and traditions before you go to Thailand, and then follow them once you arrive. Some of these rules include the following:

> Don't point your feet or fingers at religious or royal objects, which can usually be found in most buildings.
> Don't curse or make loud remarks, even if the people around you don't know what you are saying.
> Always ask the head instructor when you want to do something outside of the normal training routine, such as holding the pads for someone. It is important to always abide by the hierarchy of the gym.
> Don't walk around with a bare chest unless training in the gym or on the beach, and wear pants and long-sleeve shirts when visiting royal or government buildings.
> Bow when passing monks, religious objects, royalty, or anyone in a position of authority.

It is also important to be courteous and respectful. In Thailand, respect is offered by placing your palms together in the praying position at chin level, a motion known as Wai. The times this should be performed include:

> When you meet someone for the first time
> To the instructor anytime the instructor offers advice
> Anytime you enter or leave the ring
> To the referee before and after a fight
> To your opponents before sparring or in competition
> To all the judges and fans after a fight

Professional Fighting in Thailand

Fighting in the birthplace of Muay Thai is not an easy task to take on, and until recently few foreigners have done it and been successful. A part of the difficulty stems from the difference in rules. Although Thai boxing matches are now held in dozens of countries around the world, the rules outside of Thailand are often watered down. Some events outlaw elbow strikes or break the fighters every time they tie up in the clinch. Even though it's not hard for foreigners to schedule a fight in Thailand due to the sheer number of events that take place, it is important to understand what you are getting yourself into. Most of the native fighters have been in the game since they were children, competing every two weeks to pay for school or help support their family back home. Fighting holds a different meaning in Thailand than it does for most foreigners, so if you plan on fighting you must train hard leading up to the bout. It's not a vacation or a holiday. The consequences of stepping into a Muay Thai ring can have serious negative results if you're not ready. And before you consider fighting, you should already have a good manager and train at a gym that is concerned for your safety and finds opponents around your skill level. Listen to your instincts and trainers to know if you're ready. If you are a backpacker just coming through for a couple of weeks and think it would be cool to fight in a Muay Thai bout, you'll be in for a painful reality.

Fitness Versus Technique

In the old days when a fight fell into the hands of Thai judges, usually the most technically sound fighter received the decision. Although points are still awarded to combatants who execute beautiful moves, the fighters who constantly come forward and push the action are now earning the majority of decisions. A part of the reason for this is the spectators' thrust for action. Whether you feel this is a deterioration of the sport or a positive improvement, it stresses the need for exceptional cardio conditioning. For the duration of the fight you must be prepared to charge forward while throwing a nonstop barrage of kicks, punches, elbows, and knees. You must be prepared to take charge of long battles of tug-of-war in the clinch. You could have the best techniques in the world, but if you are getting pushed back for the majority of the fight, you'll most likely lose a judges' decision.

Wai Kru or Ram Muay

The Wai Kru or Ram Muay is a dance both Thai boxers perform in the ring just prior to battle. There is historical and cultural significance behind the ritual, but its primary purpose is to allow the fighters a chance to pay respect to their teachers. The dance begins with a unique blend of pipe and drum blaring over speakers or from a live band, giving the fighters rhythm and timing. Although every fighter has a personalized dance, both fighters will usually start in their corners and then walk the perimeter of the ring with brief pauses in each corner. This is followed by three circles around the center of the ring, where they drop down to their knees, put their hands together in the praying position, and bow three times, paying respect to their teachers and asking for protection from the spirits. Traditionally, fighters will do this while facing the direction of their home, gym, or a royal palace. As a foreigner, you will not be expected to perform the dance for your first fight, but it can be a nice way to show the crowd and judges that you respect your trainers and Muay Thai. If your trainers take the time to show you Ram Muay, it's a big honor, and you should devote an adequate amount of time to learning it properly.

The Music of Muay Thai

All fights in Thailand are accompanied by music. Sometimes a live band produces the blend of pipes, drums, and cymbals, and other times the music is broadcast over speakers. The goal of the music is to give the fighters rhythm and timing. As the pace of the music quickens with each round, the pace of the fight usually picks up as well.

Goals for Training

Creating specific goals is essential to becoming a better fighter. Short-term goals should be made on a daily and weekly basis, and it is important to pick themes. For example, one week you could decide to improve your defensive posture. While working the heavy bag on Monday, focus on keeping your hands up to protect your face. On Tuesday, concentrate on keeping your elbows tucked in to protect your ribs. If you keep your weekly goal in mind every day in training, by the end of the week you will usually notice a significant improvement. The same dedication should be offered to your long-term goals, which should be made by the month and year. If a certain technique is giving you trouble, tell yourself that you will master that technique by the end of the month. Once you have that goal established in your mind, it will make it easier to focus on that technique during training, no matter how frustrating it might be.

The more difficult techniques, such as advanced counters, should be given a year to master. If you keep your goals in mind every time you step into the gym, the weakest parts of your game could suddenly be your strongest when those twelve months are up. Going into the gym like a robot won't make you a better fighter, and every fighter, no matter how competent, has something he needs to work on. If you're not sure what part of your game is lacking, the answer is never far away. Simply ask an instructor or spar with an opponent who is better than you. Every time you enter the gym, training should be the only thing on your mind. If you remember your goals and focus on what you need to do to achieve those goals, you will be a professional in no time.

Warm Up and Cool Down

Before you begin your training sessions, it is essential that you conduct warm-up exercises and stretch to loosen up your body and get blood to your muscles. If you jump right into training without warming up and stretching, you run the risk of pulling a muscle or obtaining a more serious injury. A twenty-minute warm-up should suffice, and it could include a short run, jumping rope, shadowboxing, or all three. Stretching immediately after you have warmed up will further open up your muscles for much-needed blood and oxygen. There are thousands of different stretches, and if you don't already have a good stretching routine, there are dozens of books devoted to this subject. It is important to remember while stretching to stay relaxed, breathe steadily in through your nose and out through your mouth, not to bounce, and to hold each stretch for at least twenty seconds. If you are feeling particularly tight, hold a stretch for ten seconds, relax, take a few breaths, and then hold it for twenty seconds. Repeat each stretch until all parts of your body feel relaxed and limber. After isolating and stretching the key muscle groups, you should conduct rolling exercises to loosen your joints. These include rolling your hips as if you were using a hula hoop, making circles with your arms to loosen shoulder joints, and rotating your knees, wrists, and ankles.

Cooldown exercises and stretching after your workout are just as important. When you immediately go from training hard to sitting down and relaxing, your muscles will likely tighten and then cramp. Shadowboxing is one of the best ways to cool down because it allows you to break down the techniques you learned that day and make sure your form is perfect. Once your muscles start to relax, stretching should immediately follow.

STANCE AND FOOTWORK

Stance

All offensive and defensive Muay Thai techniques begin and end in your stance. For this reason, it is imperative that you become comfortable in your stance before you start learning anything else. It may seem awkward at first, especially if you've practiced other martial arts, but after long hours of training your body and correcting your mistakes, your stance will feel natural.

Proper stance is an ongoing debate amongst instructors, especially when they hail from different gyms. Some think you should stand more erect, while others believe you should hunch over. Some think you should remain on the balls of your feet at all times, and others feel the back foot should be planted on the ground. Some prefer a square stance, while others prefer a staggered stance. In the beginning, it's good to do exactly as your instructor tells you, but once you have spent some time in the gym and have gotten some experience, you should experiment with little adjustments such as how you position your hands to see what feels comfortable.

It takes a lot of time and hard work to acquire the stance that fits you best. Everybody is built differently, and that must be taken into consideration. A tall person with long arms is going to have a different stance than someone who is short with stubby arms. However, there are a few traits that every Muay Thai stance should have, including balanced posture, hands up for offensive techniques and defense, head tilted slightly down, shoulders up to protect the chin, and your eyes gazing at your opponent's chest so you can monitor both his upper and lower body movements. And no matter what experience level you're at, you should always spend a few minutes each day checking your stance. Even the top fighters in Bangkok will conduct quick examinations in a mirror to see if everything is where it needs to be. Your stance is your foundation, and if your foundation becomes weak, everything else will fall.

Stance Key Points

1. Every technique starts and ends in your stance.

2. There are many different stances, and some are better suited for certain situations or opponents than others.

3. It is important to acquire a stance that you feel comfortable with, but the more stances you master, the more options you'll have in a fight.

4. Constantly check your stance in the mirror to make sure you have proper form.

5. All stances should follow these basic rules:

> Balanced posture with weight distributed evenly over your hips

> Hands up and slightly out for blocking

> Feet shoulder's width apart (give or take a few inches)

> Chin tucked and shoulders up to protect your jaw

> Eyes on your opponent's chest

> Knees slightly bent

> After throwing a technique, always return to your stance

STANDARD STANCE

Chun is in a standard left lead stance, which puts his right arm and leg back in the power position. With a slightly larger percentage of his weight distributed on his front leg, he is poised on the ball of his front foot. His back foot is flat on the ground, pointed at a forty-five degree angle in relation to his opponent. His front leg is slightly bent, while his back leg is almost straight. His posture is erect, and his weight is evenly distributed above his hips. His head is hunched, allowing his shoulders to hide and protect his chin and neck. His hands are up at eye level to guard his face and head. His left hand is held half an arm's distance from his head. His right hand is close to his face, protecting his chin. His elbows are slightly bowed out so he can bring his knees underneath his elbows to check kicks. His eyes are locked on his opponent's chest.

SQUARE STANCE

Many fighters who like to kick choose a square stance over the standard stance. Having their weight more evenly distributed between their legs makes checking or kicking easier to accomplish. It also allows them to switch between a left lead and right lead stance as they move back and forth. It's a common stance that can be quite effective for those who master it, but it will open up more of your body for attack. When performing the square stance, you need to prepare for linear attacks by keeping your hands up and your guard tight. It is also important to note that when using this stance in the street you will be especially vulnerable to groin attacks.

With his left foot slightly in front of his right, Chun keeps his weight distributed evenly on both legs. His posture is erect, and both legs are slightly bent at the knee. His head is hunched, and his shoulders are up to hide and protect his chin and neck. His hands are protecting his face and head. His lead hand is held half an arm's length from his head, and his right hand is held close to his head. His arms are slightly bowed out so he can bring up his knees to the inside of his elbows to check kicks.

WEIGHT BACK

This is a stance many combatants choose to employ at one point or another during a fight. It is most commonly seen when two opponents square up in front of one another just inside kicking range. From here, you can unleash kicks with your lead leg, block or check kicks with your lead leg, or stop a quickly advancing opponent with a lead leg push kick. But when in this stance you have to be careful of attacks aimed at your rear leg, which now supports all of your weight. You can be knocked off balance very easily if caught sleeping. To be proficient at this stance, you must be prepared to move at any time. Few fighters maintain this stance for the duration of a fight; rather, they will shift back and forth between their primary stance and this one, trying to catch their opponent off guard. Fighting from this stance for an entire fight rarely results in victory.

Chun stands so that all his weight is resting on his back leg while his front foot is poised on the tips of his toes. To throw off his opponent's beat, he bounces his lead leg up and down. His back leg is slightly bent. His posture remains straight and upright. His head is hunched, allowing his shoulders to hide and protect his chin and neck. His left hand is held half an arm's length from his head, and his right hand is held six inches from his head. Chun also keeps both arms bowed slightly out so he can bring up his knees to the inside of his elbows to block kicks to his ribs or head.

SOUTHPAW STANCE

The majority of right-handed fighters will stand with their left foot forward, which puts their strong arm and leg back in the power position and allows them to throw hard punches and kicks. As can be expected, left-handed fighters often prefer to fight with their right leg forward so they too can land the hard shots with their strong side. This stance is known as southpaw. All the moves are performed the same in a southpaw stance. However, if you are fighting in a southpaw stance, the way you set up your attacks and defense will be slightly different, as will your overall fight strategy. This is also true if you are in a standard stance fighting an opponent who is in a southpaw stance. The angles from which you fire your shots will change, and you may need to take extra steps to land your attacks or use different combinations to create openings.

Taking a southpaw stance, Chun has his right leg forward. Everything else is exactly the same as the standard stance.

It is also important to remember not to drift toward your opponent's power side. When two fighters standing with their left leg forward square up, both fighters will drift to their right to avoid their opponent's power kick and punch. If one fighter has his left leg forward and the other his right, things get trickier. The fighter in a southpaw stance will want to circle to his right. The fighter in a standard stance will want to circle to his left. If they both try to circle at the same time, they will run into each other. When both fighters are experienced, what ends up happening is they each try to get their lead leg to the outside of their opponent's lead leg. It can turn into quite a battle, but the fighter who wins the battle and manages to get his lead leg to the outside of his opponent's lead leg will be in an advantageous position because his opponent's back will be partially exposed, making it easier to find openings and land clean attacks. Winning this battle is important when fighting in a southpaw stance or against an opponent in a southpaw stance.

The southpaw stance should be drilled while sparring as much as possible because you never know when you will face a southpaw in the ring. If there are no southpaws in your gym to practice with, try standing in a southpaw stance yourself. The majority of top-level Bangkok fighters can switch back and forth between a standard stance and a southpaw stance at will. It's not an easy stance to acquire if you're right-handed, and fighting from this stance should never be attempted until you have already mastered fighting from your normal stance, but becoming proficient in both stances will certainly increase your options in the ring.

Keep in mind, all the pictures in this book show a left lead fighter versus a left lead fighter (standard versus standard). All the moves are performed the same for a left lead versus right lead (standard versus southpaw), but in some cases there will be different targets, and in other cases you'll have to employ distance-covering setups to effectively land the technique. Let's use a right Thai kick to your opponent's left leg as an example. If you're in a standard stance fighting an opponent in a standard stance, your right leg will be back and his left leg will be forward. Landing the kick is a straight shot. If you're fighting a southpaw, however, his left leg is going to be back. To land a right Thai kick on his left leg from this distance you're going to have to step forward and to the side. Another option would be to target your right Thai kick to the inside of your opponent's right leg.

Chun (left) is in a southpaw stance, while his brother Somphong is in a standard stance. Chun can't circle to his left because he would be walking into his brother's power side. To get the upper hand, Chun is attempting to get his right foot to the outside of his brother's left foot, which would expose a portion of Somphong's back and make him vulnerable to attack. However, Somphong is attempting the same thing, resulting in a standoff.

Footwork

Once you've learned how to position your body in a proper Muay Thai stance, you must then learn how to move around efficiently while maintaining your stance. There are four different types of movements in Muay Thai: stepping, pivoting, sliding, and switch stepping. Whichever technique you employ, it is important that you don't get too spread out. If you get too spread out, your balance will be compromised. The same is true when you bring your feet too close together. Balance is one of the most important attributes in Muay Thai, and it can be your biggest weakness or your greatest asset. The key to obtaining excellent balance is to practice your stance and footwork so often that you instinctively know where your feet are at all times. Footwork is the root of all offensive and defensive techniques. A fighter with solid footwork is a hard fighter to hit.

Footwork Key Points

1. Balance is an attribute that must be acquired to become a proficient fighter.
2. Stay balanced on the balls of your feet for optimum mobility.
3. Feet should be a shoulder's width apart.
4. Drill footwork as much as possible.
5. Things you should never do:
    > Don't get your feet too spread out or too close together.
    > Don't position yourself so your back is to your opponent.
    > Don't crouch or lean (unless you have no other option to evade an attack).

STEPPING

When stepping, always start with the foot that is closest to the direction you want to go. If you want to move forward, start with your front foot and then follow with your back foot. It is important that the back foot covers the same ground as the front foot so you're still in your original stance. If you are moving to your left, start with your left foot and follow with your right. It is important that your stepping foot barely comes off the ground, making it appear as a slide. There are exceptions, such as when you bring your leg up to check and then step forward with that leg to execute your own attack. However, bringing your stepping foot high for the sheer sake of it will put you on one foot for that split second, which is all it takes to be struck and knocked off balance. By keeping that foot close to the ground when stepping, you maintain a solid base from which you can successfully defend attacks or launch your own attack.

PIVOTING

To execute a successful pivot, spin on the ball of one foot while the other foot swings around in a clockwise or counterclockwise direction. Your whole body should turn at the same time, and if done correctly, you will maintain your original stance. You can use either foot to pivot with, and you can also choose how far to pivot, such as a quarter or a half rotation.

Balance is the hardest thing to master when it comes to pivoting. Make sure that you stay balanced on the ball of your pivot foot and swing your hips in the direction you're pivoting while keeping your body straight and aligned. It is also important that you slide your non-pivot foot along the ground so you're not up on one foot. This will help you remain grounded and balanced.

Sometimes you may need to step out of the way of an advancing opponent and then pivot, which is a great maneuver when you're pinned against the ropes because it allows you to switch places with your opponent. In the clinch, you can use a pivot to throw your opponent or avoid attacks by pivoting out of the way. The pivot is an excellent maneuver because when done at the right moment, it almost always leaves you in a position to counter. It is not easy to master because the momentum can throw you off balance, but the benefits of having the technique in your arsenal are well worth the time it takes to master. One of the main things you should practice is not rotating too far, because it can leave you in a worse position than where you started.

Pivoting Key Points

1. Stay balanced on the ball of your grounded pivot foot.
2. Sliding your non-pivot foot along the ground allows you to stop the pivot at any time.
3. Maintain your original stance when pivoting.
4. Either foot can be used to pivot on.
5. Depending upon the situation, you can execute a quarter, half, or full rotation pivot.
6. Pivoting is usually done off a step or a slide. (Step to the outside of an opponent, and then pivot around for an attack position.)
7. Leaning over will compromise balance. Keep your body straight and aligned.
8. Pivots can be used to avoid an advancing opponent, escape from against the ropes, as a counter, or to change your angle of attack.
9. Overrotating will throw you off balance.

SLIDING

Sliding is used to cover a lot of ground in a short amount of time. A forward slide is executed by springing off your back foot, which sends your front foot gliding forward just above the ground. Instead of waiting for your front foot to land, you immediately want to follow with your back foot because otherwise the technique will leave you too spread out. Your whole body should move as one, both feet gliding over the ground in a nearly perfect stance. For a backward slide, spring off your lead foot and then follow the same rules.

Sliding is an excellent technique to land a quick attack or make a quick escape from an attack. However, it is not an easy technique to learn. At first, it might be instinctual to push off with your front foot when trying to move forward and to push off your rear foot when trying to move back. Performing it this way will make it a skip rather than a slide, and it will not be applicable in Muay Thai. Many beginners also find it hard not to jump. Although you might get away with this for a little while, eventually a good fighter will catch you in mid jump when your defenses are down. As with all techniques, it is important to constantly check your form in the mirror. You want to make sure that you're not skipping, jumping, or getting too spread out.

SWITCH STEP

A switch step is where you switch from a left lead stance to a right lead stance, or a right lead stance to a left lead stance. No substantial distance is covered in this technique; you're basically just switching your feet. It is done with a hop, but a very small one. You just want to get the bulk of your weight off the ground so you can slide your back leg up while simultaneously sliding your front leg back. Making a dramatic jump will not only telegraph your movement, but also leave both feet off the ground for a split second, making you vulnerable to attacks.

There are several reasons for employing the switch step, the most common being to get power for an attack such as a knee or kick. If you have an opening to land a kick with your lead leg, you can garner power for that kick by switch stepping it back. The kick will have to travel farther to reach its target, but it will have a lot more power upon impact. When using the switch step for an attack, however, it is important that you immediately spring into your attack after the switch because any hesitation will allow your opponent to learn your intentions and either move out of the way or put up his guard.

The switch step can also be used to avoid attacks. For example, if your opponent throws a low kick to the inside of your lead leg, you can quickly switch your stance and make him miss. This will not only throw your opponent off balance, but also put your left leg back into the power position. To make the most out of the situation, you should immediately throw a left Thai kick at your opponent before he can return to his proper fighting stance.

The switch step is also commonly used as a fake. Many fighters will switch back and forth between standard and southpaw stance to test their opponent's reactions. Sometimes you can get your opponent thinking that you are going to throw a kick with your right leg, when in actuality you are just performing a switch step. Then you throw a kick with your left leg, catching him off guard.

Stance and Footwork: Troubleshooting and Drills

When caught up in a routine, it is easy to overlook a part of your game that has steered off track. Most of the time, these problems originate from your foundation, meaning your stance and footwork. The only way to correct a problem is to realize when you're doing something wrong. This can be achieved by constantly evaluating your techniques in a mirror. It can also be achieved by asking your training partners to point out any weaknesses in your game during training or while sparring. Once you know what has gone awry, it's usually rather simple to put it back together. You just have to be willing to put in the work in the form of drills.

GETTING TOO SPREAD OUT?

A lot of fighters have a problem with getting too spread out, especially during the first year of training. It occurs most often when stepping with one foot and not making up the same amount of ground with the other, sliding one foot while leaving the other behind, or unleashing an attack or putting up a defense and not coming right back to the proper stance. No matter how it happens, this is one habit you don't want to have. Getting too spread out is a weakness any opponent will be able to capitalize on.

A helpful drill to break such a habit is to tie a length of rope between your ankles that allows your feet to move just slightly farther than a shoulder's width apart. The slack will allow you to take a step with one foot, but it will ensure that before you step again with that same foot your other foot first has to catch up. Using the rope for several training sessions should keep you from getting spread out. From that point on, break out the rope anytime you feel lengthy strides are compromising your balance.

BLIND JUMP

Sometimes practitioners get too spread out because of how they position their feet in their stance. Some simply forget to keep their feet a shoulder's width apart. If you notice that you're habitually standing with your feet too spread out, too close together, or you're simply confused about how you need to stand, stop what you're doing, close your eyes, and jump into the air as high as you can four times in a row. When you land on the last jump, look down and see where your feet are. You're going to drop one foot or the other slightly back depending on if you're right-handed or left, but the distance currently between your feet is the distance you want to keep in your stance because your instincts naturally guide you to your most balanced and steady position.

TIRE JUMP

Another helpful drill to keep you from getting too spread out is jumping on an old car tire. Before you can do this drill, you will need to locate a car tire that has a hole roughly the same diameter as your stance. Once you have one, the idea is to jump up and down on the inner edge of the tire with both feet at the same time. This will help burn into your mind the proper space that is needed between your feet because if you get too spread out, you're going to fall off. In addition, this drill will help build the muscles in your legs, improve your cardio conditioning, develop a sense of rhythm, and adequately warm up your body if you are at the beginning of your workout. Once you have mastered jumping up and down without losing your balance, you can practice your switch step. When doing this, however, it is important that you switch from jumping mode to sliding mode to avoid garnering a bad habit. Next, add punches into the mix. And if you really want a good workout, hold hand weights to help build endurance and strength in your shoulders.

JUMP ROPE

Skipping rope can be quite a challenging task if you've never done it before. Don't feel silly when starting out. Remember, everyone had to learn at one point or another. To get started, you first need to find a rope that matches your height. To gauge if a rope fits your body, stand on the middle of the rope with both feet and pull the handles up your sides. If they come up to your armpits, then it's a perfect match. When you jump, hold the handles of the rope about waist high with your hands close to your body. If you hold your hands too far out, the rope will get considerably shorter and you'll trip yourself up.

Standing in front of the rope, rotate your shoulders and wrists to get it to move over your head. When it comes down, skip over it with both feet. The goal is to jump only once per rotation, but when first starting out you might need to do a double jump until you develop good rhythm. You also don't want to jump too high because the rope might come around again before you land. To minimize the height of your jump, it helps to balance more on one foot than the other, switching your balancing side with each rotation or every other rotation. Once you get the hang of it, you can start to switch up the rhythm and move about as you skip, practicing different footwork techniques. This drill will make you faster and lighter on your feet, as well as improve your rhythm and coordination.

CHIN UP?

One of the worst habits is keeping your chin up above your shoulders where punches, kicks, and elbows can easily crash into your jaw or neck, resulting in a knockout or serious injury. Your chin is one of the most important parts of your body to protect. Many fighters will start out with their head tucked, but as the fight goes on, it will start to rise, usually because of fatigue. This can be a very dangerous habit and should be broken the moment you notice it occurring.

A good drill to get you back on track is to place a tennis ball (or any kind of ball equal in size) under your chin, and then hold it in place by pinching the ball between your chin and chest. You can do this while shadowboxing or hitting the heavy bag. When the ball falls, it lets you know that you brought your chin up too high. Like most drills, this can be very frustrating at first, chasing the ball around the gym every time you mess up, but with persistence you will quickly rid yourself of a habit that can cause unnecessary defeat.

FLAT-FOOTED?

Moving around flat-footed spells trouble because your balance will always be compromised. It is imperative that you remain on the balls of your feet while moving around because it allows you to spring into an offensive attack or into defensive mode at any moment. A good drill to see if you are moving around flat-footed is to mark your heels with chalk and then go about your shadowboxing or footwork drills. Every time you or your instructor see chalk marks on the ground you know you dropped down onto your heels. Your goal should be to try to do a three- or five-minute round of shadowboxing without making a mark on the ground. If you mess up, start the drill over, and don't stop until you can go an entire round without coming down.

WALKING A STRAIGHT LINE

When you step forward with your lead foot and then make up the ground with your rear foot, you want to be in the same stance as before you started your movement. This can often be harder than it appears. A lot of times, your rear leg will end up too far on the outside, making your stance too square. Other times, your rear foot will end too close on the inside, making your stance too staggered. A good drill to help prevent such a habit from occurring is to simply walk a straight line. That line could be a seam in a mat, tape on the floor, or a groove in cement. You want to stand so that the line runs between your legs. In the beginning it is best to take a few steps and then look down to see where your feet are, correcting your form if your feet have floated to the outside or inside. Once you have this down, try going from one end of the line to the other without looking down. If you're able to make it up and down the line time and again without your feet straying out of position, try it again while throwing straight attacks such as push kicks, straight knees, and elbows. When you make it to the end of the line, you should still be in your correct stance with the line between your legs. Next, repeat the process backward and side to side.

HANDS UP

Keeping your hands up is a must in Muay Thai because they are needed to protect your most vital assets—your head and face. Although this is a well-known fact, many fighters forget this at the worst possible moment and pay a harsh price. To combat this horrible habit, you first need to be conscious of when you're dropping your hands. One way to achieve this is to have your training partner or instructor slap you in the face every time your hands come down. You can do this while hitting the focus mitts or conducting sparring drills. After getting hit half a dozen times, your hands will miraculously stay locked in their required position. Another way is to simply stay in shape. Most fighters begin to drop their hands when fatigue sets in. First comes heavy breathing, then your muscles strain for oxygen, and then your hands feel like they're each holding a ten-pound brick. Even if you're in world-class shape fatigue can still set in, but you're going to be in much better shape to hold those bricks for the remainder of the fight. To make the most out of your hands' protection services, you should always remember to:

1. Hold your hands high enough so you can effectively block attacks to your face and head.
2. Never drop your hands when throwing a punch or bringing a punch back. Your fist should leave from and return to its exact spot in your stance. And when throwing multiple punch combinations, don't drop the hand, waiting to punch in anticipation. Keep it up to block any possible counters until the preceding punch has returned to its original position.
3. Never get lazy in the gym. Losing focus allows nasty habits to penetrate your fight game.

ATTACKS

Attack Basics

STRIKING POINTS

Targeting specific areas of your opponent's body should be a part of any fighter's game plan. Hitting one spot over and over can chop your opponent down or open up other areas to attack. Primary striking zones include your opponent's chin, temple, back of the head where the spinal cord meets the cranium, solar plexus, ribs, and the side of the leg. These will be your opponent's most vulnerable spots, as well as your most vulnerable spots. Secondary target areas are everywhere else on your opponent's body except the groin. Your reason for striking a secondary target should usually be to create an opening for one of the primary targets. The following striking points are shown in the photo:

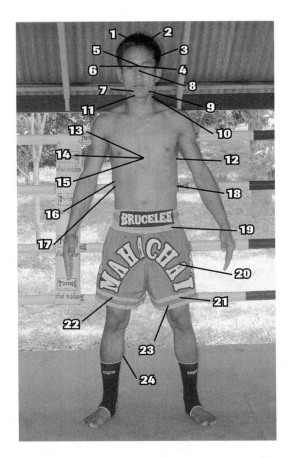

Striking Points

1. Jumping downward elbow to top of head
2. Thai kick to top of head
3. Side elbow to temple
4. Knee to face
5. Jab or cross to face
6. Overhand elbow and overhand right to face
7. Uppercut to chin
8. Push kick to face
9. Hook to chin
10. Thai kick to neck
11. Uppercut elbow to chin
12. Thai kick to ribs
13. Right cross to sternum
14. Straight knee to sternum
15. Push kick to sternum
16. Side knee to ribs
17. Hook to body
18. Thai kick to liver
19. Push kick to hip
20. Thai kick to leg
21. Push kick to front leg
22. Thai kick to rear leg
23. Thai kick to inside of lead leg
24. Thai kick to rear calf

Primary areas of attack include the chin/jaw, temple, back of head (where spinal cord meets cranium), side of legs/knees, soft portion of ribs, and the solar plexus. Weapons used to attack these targets include the shin, knee, fist, and elbow. The head is the strategic control center that directs these weapons to their appropriate targets.

BREATHING

Breathing in Muay Thai is done by inhaling through the nose and exhaling through the mouth. It is important that you take calculated breaths—breathing in and out slowly will deliver the most oxygen to your body. When throwing or absorbing a strike, you want to exhale quickly, producing the noise that you hear so often amongst Thai boxers in the ring. Holding onto your breath when striking or getting hit is a good way to get knocked out or lose your wind. The most important thing is to remember to breathe. Although breathing is a subconscious act, it's easy to tighten up and hold onto a single breath when you start out. Focusing on your breathing helps you stay relaxed, and staying relaxed helps you breathe. This is especially important to remember while in the clinch, where knees are constantly being dealt and received to the midsection. Small, quick breaths are best in the clinch because they will allow you to quickly react to your opponent's movements.

Breathing Key Points

1. Inhale through the nose and exhale through the mouth.
2. Maintain slow and steady breaths to help you stay relaxed.
3. Focus on your breath to stop any unwanted thoughts from entering your mind.
4. When throwing or receiving a strike, exhale the air in your lungs quickly.
5. Sometimes when nervous or anticipating an attack, you can forget to breathe.
6. When tired you'll naturally want to inhale through your mouth. Consciously override this by forcing yourself to take slow, deep breaths

in through your nose. Eventually you'll get enough oxygen to recover your tightened muscles.

7. Breathe with your stomach, not your chest.

8. Due to the number of blows dealt and received, it is best to take quick breaths while in the clinch so you can tighten up.

REPETITION

You can't become good at a technique by practicing it a couple of times on the heavy bag. The only way to truly grasp a technique is through repetition. The idea is to drill it so often that the movement becomes a reaction. When executing an attack, you do not want to think about how to throw the attack. If you've done painstaking repetition, the minute your mind spots an opening to launch a technique, your body will immediately execute the movement. Repetition training should be a key component of every Thai boxing training regimen. In addition to turning your techniques into instincts, it will also improve your cardio, strength, and endurance, as well as train your muscles to strike with power, accuracy, and speed.

SENSE OF DISTANCE

Sense of distance is more than knowing where you are in relation to your opponent—it's also knowing what offensive and defensive techniques you can employ at all times. Acquiring a sense of distance cannot be achieved overnight. It is earned through long hours in the gym and countless drills: hitting the heavy bag, doing padded rounds, and, most important, sparring and fighting in competition. If you've competed in Muay Thai in the past but took a substantial amount of time off, it will usually take a few weeks of drills to reacquire your sense of distance. Without training, the sense is easily lost.

TIMING

Having a sense of timing means you understand when to throw a specific strike. A good way to improve your timing is to conduct drills on the bags. When you hit the heavy bag, it will swing away from you and then come back. The trick is to hit it again before it runs into you, but this can be harder than it looks. In the beginning you will sometimes strike too early, and other times you will strike too late. But after only a few hours of practice on the heavy bag, you will begin to learn how and when to strike a moving target.

Your timing will improve even more when you begin padded rounds with a training partner or instructor. The more rounds you put in, the quicker your reactions will become. Soon, the moment your instructor or training partner holds up a pad, you'll know if you need to move forward or back to land the requested strike. This will lead you into sparring, where your timing will make leaps and bounds. You will learn how to direct your tools at the right target at exactly the right moment. You'll learn how to use a push kick to stop an advancing opponent, as well as how and when to apply all of your other offensive and defensive techniques. Expect some failure in the beginning, but stick with it. Fighters with exceptional timing will often defeat those with exceptional technique.

ACCURACY

Having tremendous speed and power will do you little good unless you can hit the target you're aiming for. Therefore, it is essential that you work to develop a sense of accuracy, which can be done by hitting the top and bottom bag and punching dummy drilling pads with an instructor or training partner, and technical sparring. When shadowboxing or hitting any piece of equipment, you should pretend a person is standing in front of you. If you don't, you'll become an expert at punching the bag and open air but nothing else. When picturing your imaginary opponent, have a mental image of the main targets, such as his face, solar plexus, and legs. These targets should always be in the back of your mind, but you don't want to become intensely focused on the target you're aiming for. In baseball, they tell pitchers to focus on throwing the ball and hitting the target. If the pitcher focuses too much on aiming, then he's not focused on throwing, which should come first. It is the same in Muay Thai. Don't think too much about the target you are trying to hit—just know where it is and then go there with the attack. Thinking and aiming will only slow you down.

Of course, this is easy to say and hard to achieve. It can get frustrating missing your mark repeatedly, but don't quit. Accuracy is something that is developed through experience, and it depends a lot upon having a steady mind when throwing your attack. Just as with timing and footwork, the more you spar and build your confidence, the better your accuracy will become. Soon you will be able to land a strike to the exact same spot over and over, slowly chopping your opponent down.

FIGHTING STRATEGY

Muay Thai is a thinking man's game and should be viewed as a chess match. In a professional bout, each opponent is looking to get several moves ahead of the other. A fighter who can mentally subdue pain and keep his cool in the hairiest of situations will have a distinct advantage. He is the one constantly breaking down his opponent's movements and patterns, searching for a weakness to capitalize on. He is the one plotting out the fight in such a way that victory will be his.

Oftentimes the majority of plotting is done in the first round. Muay Thai fights traditionally start off slow. The strikes thrown in the first round rarely have power, but causing damage is not their intent. Each fighter is testing his opponent's reactions and ability. For example, one fighter may notice that his opponent is slow to check kicks. As a result, throwing kicks will be a major component in his plot to break his opponent down. The other fighter might notice that his opponent has poor balance in the clinch, and a major component in his plot will be to break the gap, tie up, and then rack up points by executing throws or landing knees.

As the rounds progress, the fighters pick up the pace, each with his own individual goals and plots in mind. Usually the two plots are very different, but they have the same intent—victory. To prepare yourself for a fight in the ring, you should create goals and a plot while sparring opponents in the gym. If your opponent has problems checking your kicks, then you should kick as much as possible and see what else it opens up. For example, if your opponent starts dropping his hands to block your kicks, throw a right cross. If your opponent starts tying up in the clinch to stop you from kicking him, practice different methods of staying on the outside so you can maintain your strategy.

It is very easy to get sucked into your opponent's game. If he is constantly landing kicks to your leg, you'll naturally want to kick him back. But if he is a better kicker, this won't win you the fight. It is better to find his weaknesses and capitalize on them. If you can manage this, the chances are you'll eventually suck him into your game. It is also important to realize when your plot isn't working and quickly move on to a different strategy. A lot of times your opponent will catch on to your strategy and improve the weakness you have been capitalizing on. This isn't always a bad thing, because if he had a weakness to begin with, he is most likely using a fair amount of concentration to correct it, creating a weakness in another part of his game in the process. As long as you are always sharp and using your mind, you will be able to pinpoint the new chink in his armor and incorporate it into your strategy.

One of the most important things to remember is that no two fights or fighters will be the same. You must be prepared for the fighters who charge in firing. And if you're a fighter who charges in firing, you must be prepared for opponents who sit back and set everything up off your attacks. You have to know how to fight a shorter opponent, a taller opponent, and opponents who stand in an opposite stance. This can only be achieved by sparring frequently with an assortment of opponents.

Using the Ring. Using the ring as a weapon should be a part of every fighter's strategy. You can use the corner of the ring to trap your opponent. The ropes can be used to spring you forward into an attack. You can push your opponent into the ropes to spring him back into one of your attacks. If you are training at home or in a gym that doesn't have a ring, it is recommended that you search one out before a scheduled fight. The last thing you want when backing away from an attack is to be surprised by the ropes. A few weeks sparring in a ring is the minimal amount of time needed to learn your distance limitations, as well as how the ropes can be used to both your advantage and disadvantage.

Faking. Throwing fakes or feints at your opponent is an essential part of Muay Thai. You can fake a punch and then throw a kick or fake a kick and then throw a punch. Generally, faking high and going low or faking low and going high will produce the best results. The idea is to sell a technique so that your opponent moves to avoid or block it, and then unleash an attack at whichever part of his body opened up in the process. What you don't want to do is open yourself up too much with a fake. If you want to fake a jab, you don't need to throw an actual jab. All it takes is a slight clockwise jerk of your hips and a small movement of your jabbing hand to get your opponent to react. And when you fake you must always expect retaliation, so don't fake for the sheer sake of it. Faking for no reason or faking too big is a good way to get knocked out.

Practicing your fakes and experimenting with what creates openings is an important aspect of training and should be included in your daily routine. Sparring is a good time to develop fakes because you have an actual opponent to experiment with, one who won't try to knock you out if you mess up.

RANGES OF COMBAT

Ranges of combat can be talked about in theory, but in Muay Thai competition, fighters rarely stay in one range for very long. They are constantly moving back and forth between the kicking, punching, and clinching ranges, and much of the time they are somewhere between two different ranges. The chaos of movement that a fight produces can be very frustrating for a beginner. Just when he realizes he is in kicking range, his opponent moves to punching range. Just when he gets accustomed to punching range, his opponent moves to clinching range. As a beginner gains more experience, he will most likely lose focus of the three-range concept altogether. There will be just a single chaotic range of combat, but while moving around within that range, he will have a keen sense of when he can kick, punch, and engage clinch techniques. However, when first starting out it is best to focus on the four individual ranges to learn which attacks, blocks, and counters can be thrown from each.

Kicking Distance (Long Range)

If you are far enough away where you can kick your opponent, but no other strikes can be executed without sliding or stepping forward, then you are in kicking range. In Muay Thai, you strike with your shin when throwing round kicks, so the kicking range in this sport is a bit shorter than in other martial arts such as karate or kung fu. You can utilize the push kick, which is a linear attack, from a slightly greater distance because it requires striking with the ball of your foot.

Punching Distance (Mid-Range)

In the punching range you are able to throw close-range kicks, straight knees, and punches.

Clinch Distance (Close Range): Tie-Up

The tie-up position is the first clinching range. You're wrapped up with your opponent in a grapple, but there is a little bit of space between the two of you. When in this range, you can throw knees, elbows, and short punches like hooks and uppercuts. You can also execute throws.

Clinch Distance (Close Range): Smother

The second clinching range is known as the smother. This is where you are locked tightly up with your opponent, limiting you to throws, side knees, and short knees to the inside of the legs.

Kicks

Kicks are the trademark of Muay Thai. Like most martial arts, Muay Thai utilizes the push kick and side kick, both of which are mainly used as a defensive counter against an advancing opponent, to disrupt an opponent's breathing, or to set up other attacks. If you've practiced other martial arts, both will come naturally. This won't be true with the round kick or Thai kick, which is what separates the kicks of Muay Thai from the other martial arts. They are designed to cause serious damage to your opponent by driving through your target with the shinbone rather than just snapping off your target with the foot. They are not easy to master, and they can be quite painful and frustrating for someone just starting out. You must learn how to spin your hips and use the momentum the spin creates to whip your leg around into your target. After your shin drives into your opponent, you must learn how to immediately return your leg to its proper position in your stance. If you kick without using your hips, you will not do any damage. If you leave your leg hanging out there, your opponent can catch your leg or deal an attack of his own while you are off balance.

Using proper technique is a must when executing Thai kicks, but there are many different opinions when it comes to technique. Some instructors will tell you to throw your right hand down to your side as the kick goes out, and others will tell you to throw your right hand straight out. Neither is better than the other. Throwing your hand down will give you more power and speed, while throwing your hand straight out will better protect your face and midsection from counterattacks. If you choose to throw your hand down while throwing a round kick, just make sure to keep your shoulders up to protect your chin. Also, some instructors will tell you to spin all the way around when you miss your target, while others will tell you to spin only a quarter of the way around. Which you choose will depend a lot on the power of your kick. Some kicks simply have too much momentum to stop. It is important to remember that if you spin all the way around, your back will momentarily face your opponent. If he is a competent fighter, he will try to capitalize on the brief chink in your armor.

Mastering Thai kicks can take a lifetime, and there can be a lot of pain involved in the process. Anyone who practices for a decent amount of time has had a lump on his shin from colliding with his opponent's shin. Many claim that rolling Coke bottles or metal rods up and down your shins will cure injuries and make your shins tougher, but in actuality it will do more harm than good, possibly giving you arthritis down the road. Although traditionally fighters kicked banana trees, it was done out of necessity rather than practicality. Most gyms have switched to heavy bags now that they are cheaper and more readily available. The best way to toughen your shins is through countless repetitions on the bags, sparring, and competition fighting. When the inevitable lump forms on your shin, it should be treated with boxing liniment and care.

Kicking Key Points

1. Spin on the ball of your foot when executing round kicks.
2. Throw kicks through your target.
3. Stay balanced.
4. For round kicks, always spin your hips in a circular direction.
5. Keep as erect as possible, don't lean forward or backward.
6. Unless you're moving into another technique that requires you to step forward, immediately return your leg back to its position in your stance after kicking.
7. Stay relaxed.

REAR LEG THAI KICK TO LEAD LEG

The low Thai kick can produce devastating results when thrown at the right time and at the right spot. The aim is to hit your opponent in the nerve that runs down the outside of his thigh. A good low-kicker will target this spot again and again, until his opponent can barely stand. The technique is frequently used by good punchers because they can switch back and forth between low attacks and high attacks, confusing their opponent in the process. In the kicking range the technique works great to counter an opponent coming straight in, but it is best utilized in the punching range because it fits so well into punching combinations. When in the punching range, however, you may have to slide-step to the side to connect properly, especially when fighting southpaws.

Chun (left) is in a proper Muay Thai stance, searching for an opening on his brother Somphong.

Chun unleashes a right low Thai kick to the nerve running down the outside of Somphong's lead thigh. Chun started the movement by pushing off the ball of his right foot, while at the same time snapping his hips in a counterclockwise direction. To help his hips rotate, Chun throws his left shoulder back. His left hand is protecting his face, and he throws his right hand out to keep his brother from closing the gap. His right shoulder is kept high to protect his chin. He is balanced on the ball of his left foot as his rotating hips whip his leg around into the target.

FRONT LEG THAI KICK TO INSIDE LEG

Although this kick can inflict damage on our opponent, it generally doesn't have as much power as a low rear leg kick to the outside of your opponent's leg. If your opponent is placing a larger percentage of his weight on his lead leg, you can use this

Chun (left) is in a proper Muay Thai stance, searching for an opening on his brother Somphong.

From his stance, Chun snaps his hips in clockwise direction, pulling his right shoulder back to help the rotation. The momentum of his rotating hips whips Chun's left leg toward the inner thigh of Somphong's lead leg. To check his distance, he throws his left arm straight out. His left shoulder is protecting his chin, and his right hand is up guarding his face. After his shin makes contact with the soft tissue just above Somphong's knee, Chun quickly retracts his kick and returns to his stance.

kick to off-balance him and set yourself up for a more devastating attack. When executed from the punching range, it is speedy and easy to land. A lot of fighters will use this technique heavily in the first round to judge distance and test their opponent's reactions. When throwing it from the kicking range, you'll often have to take a step forward for your kick to land, but this can be risky because if your opponent sees the kick coming, he can simply step his lead leg back, make you miss, and then counter with an attack of his own. In the later, action-packed rounds, it is almost always thrown as part of a combination. It is most commonly used as a setup for a right cross.

FRONT LEG THAI KICK TO BACK LEG

This technique is very hard to execute directly from your stance. Because you're attacking your opponent's rear leg, you'll usually have to cover some distance to land the kick. The most common method to break the distance is to slide to the side, as demonstrated in the photo. Although the kick is a power blow, it doesn't pack as much wallop as a kick from your power side, and it rarely ends a fight. However, it is great for setting up other techniques because it changes the angle at which you're facing your opponent. It can also be an elusive move when done properly. The first step in the technique can make your opponent think you're about to throw a Thai kick with your rear leg, causing him to either bring up his front leg to check or shift his weight back to prepare for impact. If your opponent does either, your kick is sold. By finishing the move, you'll catch your opponent off guard and land a kick to his rear leg. It is important to note that the steps shown in the photos should be done in rapid succession without any hesitation.

Chun (right) is in a proper Muay Thai stance, searching for an opening on his brother Somphong.

Chun slides to his left by pushing off the ball of his right foot. As his left foot slides over the canvas, his right foot immediately follows so he doesn't get too spread out. Somphong is looking down, anticipating a kick from Chun's rear leg.

Chun steps forward with his right foot. The moment his foot touches down, he wastes no time whipping his hips around in a clockwise direction, throwing his right shoulder back and pushing off his left foot to help the rotation. While spinning on the ball of his right foot, Chun stays protected by keeping his right hand up by his face and tucking his chin behind his left shoulder. Thrusting his left arm out for balance and checking, he crashes his shin into the nerve running down the outside of Somphong's rear thigh.

REAR LEG THAI KICK TO MIDSECTION (TWO RANGES)

When it comes to Thai kicks to the midsection, the ribs and stomach are the primary destinations. There are two ranges from which Thai kicks to the midsection can be thrown. The first is from the standard kicking range. From this range, your kick will usually be targeted at your opponent's ribs, and your leg should be fully extended when your shin makes contact. The second midsection Thai kick can be thrown from punching range. From this range, your leg will be bent considerably, and your target will generally be your opponent's stomach. Both are effective kicks, and which one to throw depends entirely upon your distance from your opponent. A good fighter can throw a long-range Thai kick to his opponent's ribs and then switch to a short-range Thai kick to the stomach if his opponent should quickly move forward. This is a good skill to acquire due to the chaotic movements and distances that are characteristic of any fight.

Rear Leg Thai Kick to Midsection from Kicking Range

Somphong (left) is in a proper Muay Thai stance, searching for an opening on his brother Chun. In this version, Somphong throws his right arm down to his side rather than straight out. This adds more power to the kick but leaves him more vulnerable to a counterattack.

Somphong pushes off his right foot and throws his left shoulder back to help whip his hips in a counterclockwise direction. Just as with the low kick, the rotation of his hips whips his right leg off the ground. Rotating on the ball of his left foot, he casts his straightened leg into the unprotected organs just below Chun's ribs.

Rear Leg Thai Kick to Midsection from Punching Range

Chun (left) is in a proper Muay Thai stance, searching for an opening on his brother Somphong.

Somphong tries to close the distance, and Chun spots his opening. To begin his midsection Thai kick from punching range, he pushes off the ball of his right foot and throws his left shoulder back to help whip his hips in a counterclockwise direction. His left hand guards his face, and his right shoulder shields his jaw. He throws his right hand straight out to maintain proper distance between him and Somphong. Because his brother is so close, he keeps his kicking leg bent rather than straight, digging his shin into Somphong's liver and stomach upon impact. From here, Chun will push off Somphong's body with his kicking leg to create distance between them and return to his normal stance.

FRONT LEG THAI KICK TO MIDSECTION (THREE VARIATIONS)

There are several different ways you can throw a rib kick with your lead leg. If you're already within range, you can simply fire the kick off from your normal fighting stance. It usually won't cause much damage, but it can be used to set up other attacks or simply catch your opponent off guard. If you want the kick to be devastating, you will want to first switch your feet. If you have enough distance between you and your opponent, you can just take a step forward with your back leg, putting your front leg in the power position. If you don't have such room to play with, you can perform a switch step and then immediately fire off the kick. Whichever technique you employ, it is important that you always return your leg to its proper position in your stance after the kick. However, a lot of times the momentum of the recovery will cause you to step back, putting you in a south-paw stance, in which case you'll need to take a step to reacquire your original stance.

Front Leg Thai Kick to Midsection from Stance. This kick does not pack nearly as much of a wallop as a Thai kick executed with the rear leg, but it is still highly effective due to its quickness and convenience. It's great for countering punches, catching an opponent coming in, or to set up another technique. It works best when followed by a push kick so you can maintain your distance.

Chun (left) is in a proper Muay Thai stance, searching for an opening on his brother Somphong.

Without switching his feet, Chun throws his right shoulder back to help whip his hips in a clockwise direction. His spinning hips pull his left leg off the ground and whirl it toward his target. It is important to note that his kicking leg makes a circular path, not a linear one. His kicking leg is bent due to the short distance between him and his opponent, and his shin (not his foot) makes contact with Somphong's liver and stomach.

Lead Leg Thai Kick to Midsection off Step. This technique is best used when there is too much distance between you and your opponent to land the kick. By stepping forward with your back foot, you're not only going to close the distance, but also drop your lead leg back into the power position. Whether doing the technique off a check or simply as a step, you want to make sure it is executed as one fluid movement.

Chun (left) is in a proper Muay Thai stance, searching for an opening on his brother Somphong.

With too great a distance between him and his brother to land a lead Thai kick to the ribs, Chun slides his right foot forward, which puts his left leg in the power position.

Chun pushes off with his left foot and throws his right shoulder back to help spin his hips in a clockwise direction. His right hand is guarding his face, and his left shoulder is protecting his chin. He keeps his kicking leg bent due to the short distance between him and his brother. Upon impact, his shin digs into his brother's stomach and liver.

Lead Leg Thai Kick to Midsection off Switch Step. Performing a switch step before throwing a lead Thai kick will help you gain power, but it can also be used to throw your opponent off with a sudden switch of stance. This maneuver should be done quickly and without letting your feet leave the canvas. You don't want to jump or hop when you switch your feet because it will compromise your balance. It is best used when in kicking range or to counter an incoming attack.

Chun (left) is in a proper Muay Thai stance, searching for an opening on his brother Somphong.

Chun switches his stance by quickly reversing the position of his feet, putting him into a southpaw stance. As he does this, he makes sure not to jump and that his feet land a shoulder's width apart.

Chun pushes off the ball of his left foot and throws his right shoulder back to help spin his hips in a clockwise direction. While spinning on the ball of his left foot, his right hand guards his face and his left shoulder protects his chin. Chun's kicking leg is bent due to the short distance between him and his brother. Upon impact, his shin digs into his brother's stomach and liver.

HEAD KICK

Kicking the head is probably the most desired technique because of its effectiveness and beauty. The idea is to catch an unsuspecting opponent with his hands down with a kick to the jaw, side of the neck, or back of the head or grazing the temple. Landing a clean kick to any of these targets will have devastating results. Throwing this kick without an opening, however, can be dangerous. When you throw a head kick your shin has to travel a very long distance, making it the easiest kick to counter. It's best used after landing several clean rib kicks because many opponents will begin to drop their hands in anticipation, allowing you to go high. But if you don't have good flexibility, attempting this kick will do little more than throw you off balance.

Rear Leg Thai Kick to Head

Somphong (left) is in a proper Muay Thai stance, searching for an opening on his brother Chun.

Somphong pushes off the ball of his right foot and throws his left shoulder back to help whip his hips in a counterclockwise direction. His left hand is protecting his face, and his right shoulder guards his chin. Spinning on the ball of his left foot, he keeps his kicking leg straight. Because he is targeting his brother's neck, he has to bring his right leg up over his brother's shoulder and then down to his target, connecting with the inside of his shin.

JUMPING (FLYING) KICK

Everyone loves to see flying kicks. Although they are considered flashy moves, they can be extremely effective when done with proper form and at the right moment. A good time to pull off a flying kick is when you have your opponent on the run, because he is backing up and doesn't have the balance or footing to counter while you're in the air. An even better time to throw one is when your opponent is backing up into the ropes. Just as the ropes spring your retreating opponent back toward the center of the ring, you want to crash into him with the flying kick, doubling the impact. It's always a risky maneuver because both of your feet will be off the ground. If your opponent manages to hit you, it will usually result with you lying on your back. And if you miss, you won't be able to stop your momentum, which might open your opponent up for a counterattack. There is even a chance you might fly out of the ring.

On a technical side, flying kicks are thrown almost like normal Thai kicks. The only difference is you're going to crouch down a little and then explode forward and upward off the ball of your rear foot. You're still generating power for the kick by whipping your hips around, and you still need to keep your guard up. Flying kicks work best when directed at either the ribs or head.

LEAD LEG PUSH KICK

In Muay Thai, the lead leg push kick is the equivalent to the boxer's jab. It is used to judge distance, set up other techniques, or stop an advancing opponent. A normal lead leg push kick packs enough wallop to cause pain to your opponent or disrupt his breathing. And if landed with enough power and on the right spot, a push kick can occasionally knock your opponent out. The kick should be thrown with power and speed, but you have to be careful not to fall forward into the kick. Even if you miss, you want to retract your kick in the air and then drop your kicking foot back to its proper place in your stance. If you fall forward into the kick and your opponent throws an attack, you're going to get hit twice as hard. The best way to avoid this is to always focus on your technique. When starting out, many people will simply lift their foot up to the target and then try to push their opponent away. This has little to no effect. To throw a proper push kick, you first want to lift your knee up toward your chest. Keeping your knee stuck to your chest, you then bring up your foot. Once your foot is on the same plane as your knee and the target, you finally thrust out your kicking leg using your hips. It is important that your grounded foot maintain a proper base as you do this. When you connect with your kick, you want to push your opponent back, not the other way around.

You can use the ball of your foot, heel, or your whole foot to make contact with your target. Most of the time you'll want to use the ball of your foot because it will increase the range of your attack. It will also cause the most pain because of the small surface area of your weapon. Using the heel or whole foot comes into play when there is only a small distance separating you and your opponent, such as in punching range. It doesn't cause as much pain as striking with the ball because of the increased surface area of your weapon, but it tends to be more powerful and you'll have less of a chance of missing when the whole foot is involved.

Although fighters often throw the push kick to their opponent's hip, middle thigh, stomach, and neck, there are three main targets professionals will aim for time and again—the head, midsection, and knee. Kicking the knee is a good way to stop proficient punchers. It's also a wonderful technique to knock your opponent off balance. While your opponent is still wobbling, worried about another low kick, you have an opening to go high with your next attack. This maneuver works best when you throw the kick down into your opponent's knee rather than straight at it because it will force your opponent's head to drop into your follow-up attack. This can be achieved by lifting your knee as if you were going to target your opponent's midsection, and then angling and thrusting the kick downward into your opponent's knee.

A push kick to the midsection is best used to push your opponent back and create distance or to stop your opponent's attack. The best target is the sternum, and when done fast and with power, it can successfully knock the air from your opponent. Just like the push kick to the knee, this technique should be done by first lifting your knee up to the chest and then thrusting the hips forward. After the kick, you should bring your leg back to its proper position in your stance. It is very important when executing this maneuver that you don't fall into your kick because if you miss your target, which is quite common, you could fall right into your opponent's attack.

Push kicks to the face are more difficult to pull off because of the distance your weapon has to travel. But because Thai boxers often hold their hands apart in an open guard, it can certainly be landed. And when landed to the face, this kick has knockout power. If you're fighting a Thai opponent, you're not going to become his friend by doing this, especially if the bottom of your foot just grazes his face. In Thai culture, pointing the bottom of your feet toward someone is considered rude and disrespectful, and Thai boxers do not like to lose face. Nevertheless, it's still done often, causing many fights to become savagely aggressive as a result. If your opponent is walking forward with a wide-open guard, it is simply too good an opportunity to pass up.

Somphong (left) is in a proper Muay Thai stance, searching for an opening on his brother Chun.

Whether Somphong is going to throw a lead leg push kick to Chun's leg, sternum, or face, he must first lift his front knee toward his chest to generate power.

Trying to disrupt Chun's balance so he can follow up with a punch, Somphong directs his push kick at the middle of the thigh. He does this by thrusting his kicking leg out using his hips and making contact with the ball of his foot.

To knock the wind from Chun and drive him back, Somphong aims his push kick at the midsection. Just as with the kick to the knee or thigh, he thrusts his kicking leg out using his hips and makes contact with the ball of his foot.

Spotting a gap in Chun's guard, Somphong targets his push kick at the face. Once again, he thrusts his kicking leg forward using his hips and makes contact with the ball of his foot.

REAR LEG PUSH KICK

Executing a push kick with your rear leg creates more power, but it is going to take more time to land due to the distance it has to travel, making it easier for your opponent to spot. There are two versions of the rear leg push kick. The first resembles the lead leg push kick in that you want to thrust your leg straight out to your target and then bring it straight back into your stance. The second version is to keep your kicking leg slightly bent at an angle, catching your opponent across the hips with all of your foot. It is best utilized to push your opponent back while in the punching range. It's also harder to miss because you're striking with your entire foot.

Somphong (left) is in a proper Muay Thai stance, searching for an opening on his brother Chun.

To generate power, Somphong lifts his right knee toward his chest.

Thrusting his kick forward using his hips, Somphong drives his kick into Chun's left hip. Using his entire foot to lessen his chances of missing, he pushes Chun out of punching range.

SIDE KICK

The side kick is hard to land on a moving opponent, and as a result it isn't used that often in professional Thai boxing matches. You will see it most often when a fighter misses a Thai kick and is left with his side exposed. With little time to scramble back into his stance before his opponent lands an attack, he throws the side kick, basically countering his opponent's counter. It can pack a lot of power if done with good technique and at the proper time, often sending your opponent flying across the ring.

Chun (left) is in a proper Muay Thai stance, searching for an opening on his brother Somphong.

Just like with the push kick, Chun has to first bring up his knee to spring-load his leg before unleashing his kick to the midsection.

Thrusting with his hips, Chun drives the whole of his foot into Somphong's stomach, pushing him back and stopping any attack he might have launched.

Punches

Although punching isn't scored very highly on the judges' scorecards, Thai boxers today realize the importance of having a good boxing game and work to master striking with their hands. A Thai boxer with good punching skills will use jabs and crosses to set up kicks, as well as transition from punching range into the clinch where he can fire off elbow and knee strikes. Many Thai boxers who receive savage cuts during a bout will shift entirely into punching mode in an attempt to knock their opponent out before the referee stops the fight. Statistically, most knockouts in Thai boxing matches come by way of a punch or elbow strike.

To develop good punching skills you must isolate your hands in training to develop proper technique. Most Muay Thai gyms incorporate a boxing session into their weekly program where students train on the focus mitts with an instructor or spar one another using only their hands. You can also isolate and improve your handwork while shadowboxing or hitting the heavy bag, top and bottom bag, and speed bag. Drilling is important because just like all techniques in Muay Thai, boxing is complicated and difficult to master. It takes a lot of practice to not only be able to throw with speed, accuracy, and power, but also use your hands fluidly along with your other tools. There is a reason why an entire combative art has been devoted to just punching.

However, the techniques of Western boxing are significantly different than those of Muay Thai. Western boxers tend to place a larger percentage of their weight over their back leg. They remain in a somewhat crouched position to bob and weave, and when throwing a punch, they tend to twist or rotate their body dramatically. These are all excellent techniques for boxing, but they don't translate very well to Muay Thai competition, where lightning-fast kicks and knees come at you from many angles. Thai boxers stand more upright because it allows them to better defend attacks aimed at their lower body, as well as launch their own attacks with their knees and legs. Thai boxers tend not to bob and weave because it is a good way to eat a knee or kick to the face. Thai boxers tend to throw punches with their shoulder rather than making dramatic rotations with their body because it allows them to follow up with their other tools, such as kicks. It is good to learn Western boxing, but you have to remember to adapt to the situation. If you are just boxing, you will probably want to use a boxing stance. If you are sparring with Muay Thai rules or want to compete in a Muay Thai competition, you want to use the Thai boxing stance and Thai boxing techniques.

Punching Key Points

1. Punching in Muay Thai comes more from the shoulder and hips than the legs. Don't exaggerate the punch by turning your foot or dropping your weight.
2. Use your shoulder and the twist of your hips to throw and retract punches like a bullwhip.
3. You should snap into your targets rather than push against them. If the heavy bag swings away when you hit it, you're probably pushing your punches. The bag should hop in place when punched correctly.
4. For added snap, your punching hand should stay relaxed until just before impact.
5. To develop snapping punches, you must put a lot of rounds into shadowboxing, the top and bottom bag, the speed bag, training on the focus mitts, and sparring drills.
6. Punches always start and end in the same spot. Don't drop your hand down on the way back from the target.
7. When punching, don't let your arms float out to the sides. It takes away power and makes you more vulnerable to counterattacks. Keeping your punches straight allows you to harness the power in your hips.

JAB

Your jab will be the cornerstone of your boxing game, and it should primarily be used to set up kicks, knees, elbows, or other punches. When an opponent comes at you with a combination, the jab, because of its simplicity, speed, and straight

Shifting his weight slightly forward, Chun lashes out with the jab, using his shoulder to generate power. As his arm extends, he rotates his fist over forty-five degrees so that his palm is facing down. He tightens up his fist just before impact, striking Somphong's chin with the knuckles of his index and middle fingers. He keeps his right hand up to protect his face from possible counters.

line of attack, can temporarily disrupt your opponent's attack and rhythm, allowing you to follow the jab with a much more powerful attack. There are many different ways to execute the jab and many different angles from which to throw a jab, but it's still the easiest punch to acquire. It will also be the handiest. Other than your front leg push kick, your jab will be your closest weapon to your opponent.

STRAIGHT JAB

The straight jab is best used off a slide to cover distance and break through your opponent's guard. It has a lot more power than the standard jab because you're using your shoulder, hip, and forward momentum to throw the punch. And because you

Shifting his weight slightly forward, Chun rotates his hips in a clockwise direction and throws his left arm straight out. It is important to note that he doesn't turn his hand over as he did when executing the standard jab. Coming in with stealth and power, his fist penetrates through his brother's guard. His right hand remains up to protect the right side of his face, and his chin is tucked safely behind his left shoulder.

are not turning your hand over as you do with the standard jab, it creates a hard-to-read angle that can sneak through your opponent's guard and knock him back, allowing you to unleash with a follow-up attack.

CROSS

The cross is probably the second most important punch in Muay Thai. It almost always follows the jab in the classic one-two combination, and it is responsible for the majority of knockouts by way of punches. Despite its effectiveness, it is harder to land than the jab because it starts from farther away, making it easier to spot. A good cross can be a perfect counter for a Thai kick, but if you're not quick with the punch, you're going to eat the kick.

Shifting a greater portion of his weight to his front leg, Chun turns his hips and shoulders in a counterclockwise direction, spinning on the ball of his left foot while keeping his back leg straight. With his right fist shooting straight out, Chun keeps his chin tucked behind his right shoulder and his left hand up to guard his face. As the punch nears Somphong's chin, Chun tightens his fist and turns his hand over so his palm is facing the ground. He strikes Somphong's chin with the knuckles of his index and middle fingers.

CROSS TO THE BODY

If you're always throwing punches at your opponent's head, he will most likely make it a point to keep his hands up for protection. A good cross to the body will switch things up and keep your opponent guessing. And if it is a stern cross to the body, it will knock the air out of your opponent and possibly create openings for other attacks. It is important not to drop your head low to deliver this punch, but rather throw your strike downward from within your proper stance. If your opponent is considerably shorter than you and you can't reach your target while maintaining your stance, stay erect but lower your elevation by bending your front knee. Leaning down into the punch is a good way to catch a knee to the face.

Shifting a larger portion of his weight onto his front leg, Chun turns his hips and shoulders in a counterclockwise direction. At the same time, he bends his front leg to lower his elevation but keeps his posture erect. He rotates on the ball of his front foot to generate power, but he keeps his back leg straight. He makes sure to keep his chin tucked behind his right shoulder and his left hand up to guard his face. As his punch nears Somphong's solar plexus, he turns his hand over so his palm is facing the ground and tightens up his fist. He makes contact with the knuckles of his index and middle fingers.

HOOK

Because of the angle at which it is thrown, the hook can often catch your opponent by surprise. It can also lead to a knockout when done correctly and landed clean. It is a versatile punch because it can be thrown from the clinching range, which will require your arm to bend at a forty-five degree angle, or thrown from the punching range, which will require your arm to be just slightly bent. It can be effective to throw it as a single punch, but it works best off other hand techniques such as the cross. It's an excellent technique to use as a counterpunch on an advancing opponent, as well as a good attack to open up an opponent for another hand technique. It is important that you don't draw your fist dramatically back when executing this punch—it is a hook, not a haymaker. Making a big, looping path with your fist will allow your opponent to see it coming and counter with a straight punch long before your fist reaches its target.

Long Hook

Shifting a larger portion of his weight to his front leg, Chun rotates his hips in a clockwise direction. Instead of throwing his punch straight as he would with a jab or a cross, he uses the momentum of his hips to cast his fist on a circular path. His arm is bent, and he keeps his elbow and fist at the same elevation as his target. His chin is tucked behind his left shoulder, and his right hand is up protecting his face.

Short Hook

Chun begins the close hook the same way he did the long hook, by shifting a larger portion of his weight to his front leg and rotating his hips in a clockwise direction. While swinging his fist on a circular path, he lifts his elbow up so that it is at the same elevation as his fist and the target. He keeps his right hand up to protect his face, and his left shoulder protects his chin.

UPPERCUT

The uppercut is most commonly used while in clinching range, but it can be equally effective from a greater distance when thrown immediately after a jab or a cross. It should be executed with speed and power, giving it knockout capabilities. It is most effective when entering or breaking out of the clinch. Rarely do fighters open a combination with an uppercut, because of the visible angle from which it is thrown and the short distance it can cover. Western boxers will frequently dip down before throwing an uppercut, but you have to be careful doing this in Muay Thai because you might catch a knee to the face. It is best to throw it right from your stance, using your shoulders and hips instead of your legs to generate power.

Turning his hips slightly in a clockwise direction, Chun drops his lead arm slightly and then uses the power of his shoulder to spring his fist up into Somphong's jaw. His right hand guards his face, and his left shoulder protects his chin.

OVERHAND

The overhand is best used as a counterpunch or immediately following another hand technique such as an uppercut. It packs plenty of power and speed, but due to the odd angle of attack, it is sometimes difficult to land clean on your opponent's jaw. If your opponent is an experienced practitioner and sees the overhand coming, he can block the strike by dipping his head down. The result will usually be your fist crashing into the top of his skull, which can easily break your hand. For this reason, it is best to set it up. When your opponent throws a jab, you can slip to the side of his punch and then bring your overhand punch over the top of his jab. Your timing has to be exact, but if your punch finds its target on an advancing opponent, there is a good chance you're going to knock him out. It is thrown much like a cross, except your fist is going to make an upward arc into your opponent's jaw. It's almost like you're executing a freestyle swimmer's stroke with one hand.

To throw the overhand right, Chun shifts a greater portion of his weight forward and turns his hips in a counterclockwise direction. His back leg is straight, and his front leg is bent into the punch. Pulling his left shoulder down, he sends his right fist in an upward arc toward Somphong's jaw, a movement that resembles a freestyle swimmer's stroke. Keeping his left hand up to protect his face and shielding his chin behind his right shoulder, he turns his hand over so that the knuckles of his index and middle fingers land flush into Somphong's jaw.

Elbows

Out of all the techniques a Thai boxer has in his arsenal, elbows are by far the most feared because a clean blow frequently results in a knockout or a cut. The cuts caused by an elbow tend to be much longer and deeper than those caused by a punch, and although they eventually heal, they can leave pockets of scar tissue that will be targeted by opponents in future bouts, opening upon the slightest impact. For this reason, elbow strikes are commonly outlawed in Muay Thai events outside of Thailand, changing the sport dramatically.

Despite their danger, elbows are as much of a part of Thai boxing as any other technique, and those who claim they are too dangerous don't fully understand the sport. With two experienced combatants, landing a clean elbow is a difficult task due to the short range of the weapon. They are most common in the clinch, but while in the clinch your arms are usually wrapped up with your opponent, pushing and pulling for position. Finding an opening to throw an elbow is difficult to say the least. Fighters known for elbow strikes usually have masterful setups or impeccable timing, catching an opponent the moment he drops his hands.

There are two ways to utilize elbow strikes: catch your opponent with the blunt of your elbow, which will most likely lead to a knockout, or graze your opponent's face with the tip of your elbow, which will most likely open a cut. If you open a cut on your opponent, the ringside doctor will have to examine the damage before the fight can continue. If the doctor decides the cut is too deep, you will be declared the winner by technical knockout (TKO). If the doctor clears your opponent, the tempo of the fight will most likely increase. Your opponent will know that the doctor is watching him carefully and the fight can be stopped at any moment. He knows that he is covered in blood, which doesn't look good in the eyes of the judges, and that he now has a weakness you can capitalize on, jabbing at his cut to open it even more. For these reasons, he will most likely come forward blazing, trying to get a knockout while at the same time trying to protect his cut from further abuse. If it is you who received the cut, you should probably use a similar strategy unless you are confident that you can win based on the points you have already scored.

Having flexibility in your shoulders is a must for throwing proficient elbows, which is why skinnier fighters and women generally have better elbow strikes. Like all techniques in Muay Thai, your hips generate the majority of the power for the strike. Whether you land your shot or miss, you mustn't let your elbow hang out there, because your opponent will most likely retaliate with an elbow of his own. You want to lash out with the strike and then return your elbow to its proper place in your stance as quickly as possible.

In competition, elbows are priceless and should not be ignored. There are many fragile bones in your hand that can shatter when striking someone in the face. Such injuries can take months, if not years, to heal. Striking with the elbow on the other hand may cause bruising or pain, but it won't end your career or do any permanent damage. The majority of damage will be done to your opponent, which should be the goal of any strike. Professional Thai boxers callus their elbows by constantly practicing them on the heavy bag, focus mitts, and Thai pads. After years of executing such drills on a daily basis, they can unleash elbow strikes with no worry of causing damage to themselves.

SIDE ELBOW

The side elbow is responsible for more knockouts than all of the other elbow strikes combined. It is much like the hook in that it is cast from the side and crashes into your opponent's jaw or temple. And just like the hook, it packs quite a wallop. For a knockout you generally want to make contact with the hard part of your forearm just below the elbow, but if your intent is to open a cut, you should graze your opponent's face with the tip of your elbow. It is best used in the clinch, but usually you'll have to set it up by pulling one of your opponent's arms down to open a gap for the elbow to slip through. You can also set it up with a flurry of punches that ends with an elbow to the jaw or by intercepting or countering an anxious opponent who comes in with his hands down.

Left Side Elbow (Front View)

Chun is demonstrating the proper technique for the left side elbow. His left arm is bent and level with his shoulder. His right arm is up, acting as a barrier for counters and protecting the right side of his face. His chin is buried under his left shoulder. Chun's elbow attack, as shown, is at the end of its course. It's important that you don't throw it any farther because a miss would expose an opening in your guard.

Left Side Elbow (Attack View)

Distributing his weight forward, Somphong rotates his hips in a clockwise direction and turns on the ball of his lead foot. His elbow rises up to the level of his target, and then it travels on a circular path into the target. Keeping his right hand up to protect his face and his chin tucked behind his left shoulder, he uses his left shoulder and hips to drive the tip of his elbow into Chun's jaw.

This same attack can be executed at a closer range, but instead of using the tip of the elbow, you will use the hard part of your forearm just below your elbow. It is just as effective and devastating a blow.

Right Side Elbow (Front View)

Chun is demonstrating the proper technique for the right side elbow. His right arm is bent and level with his shoulder. His left arm is up, acting as a barrier for counters and protecting the left side of his face. His chin is buried under his left shoulder. Chun is also turning his hips—like throwing a right cross—to gain power and cover the distance needed to land the strike. Chun's elbow attack, as shown, is at the end of its course. It's important that you don't throw it any farther because a miss will open a weakness in your guard.

Right Side Elbow (Attack View)

Somphong (left) is in a proper Muay Thai stance, searching for an opening on his brother Chun.

In order to land a right side elbow attack, Somphong first needs to create an opening. He does this by trapping Chun's left arm with his left hand and pulling it down and away from Chun's face.

Now that he has created an opening, Somphong distributes a larger portion of his weight on his front foot and turns his hips in a counterclockwise direction to gain power, speed, and momentum for the strike, as well as to help cover the distance needed to execute the attack. Spinning on the ball of his left foot, he uses his circular momentum and shoulder to drive the tip of his right elbow into Chun's jaw.

This same attack can be executed at a closer range, but instead of using the tip of the elbow, you will use the hard part of your forearm just below your elbow. It is just as effective and devastating a blow.

CIRCULAR ELBOW (OVER-THE-TOP)

The circular, over-the-top elbow is responsible for most of the cuts that come by way of elbow strikes because it is deployed at a downward angle, causing the tip of the elbow to crash into the tissue just above your opponent's eyes, which happens to be the easiest part of the face to open up. It is one of the simplest elbows to land because it comes over the top of your opponent's hands. Even if your opponent has his hands up, it will be hard for him to stop all of the downward momentum in your attack. Sometimes all it takes is just a graze to open a cut that can stop the fight. It is known as the circular elbow because of how your shoulders rotate.

Left Over-the-Top Elbow (Front View)

Chun is demonstrating the proper technique for the left over-the-top elbow. His left forearm is angled down, while his elbow is raised high. His right arm is up, acting as a barrier for counters and protecting his face. His left shoulder is shielding his chin.

Left Over-the-Top Elbow (Attack View)

Somphong (left) is in a proper Muay Thai stance, searching for an opening on his brother Chun.

Rotating his left shoulder, Somphong brings his left elbow high and angles his forearm down. At the same time, he uses his left hand to trap Chun's right hand. Pulling Chun's hand down and away from his face creates an opening for the elbow strike.

Shifting a larger portion of his weight to his right side, Somphong turns his hips in a clockwise direction and rotates on the ball of his left foot. With his right hand protecting his face and his left shoulder shielding his chin, he uses the power in his left shoulder and the momentum of his hips to drive his elbow down, crashing the tip into the soft tissue just above Chun's eye socket.

Right Over-the-Top Elbow (Front View)

Chun is demonstrating proper technique for the right over-the-top elbow. His right elbow is up, and his forearm is angled down. His left arm is up, acting as a barrier for counters and protecting the left side of his face. His right shoulder shields his chin.

Right Over-the-Top Elbow Strike (Attack View)

Somphong (left) is in a proper Muay Thai stance, searching for an opening on his brother Chun.

Rotating his right shoulder, Somphong brings his right elbow high and angles his forearm down. At the same time, he uses his right hand to trap Chun's left hand. Pulling Chun's left hand down and away from his face creates an opening for the elbow attack.

Shifting a larger portion of his weight to his left side, Somphong turns his hips in a counterclockwise direction and rotates on the ball of his right foot. With his left hand protecting his face and his right shoulder shielding his chin, he uses the strength in his right shoulder and the momentum of his hips to drive his elbow down, crashing the tip into the soft tissue just above Chun's eye socket.

UPPERCUT ELBOW

The uppercut elbow can be thrown straight up at a ninety-degree angle or up at a forty-five degree angle, and deciding which angle to choose depends upon how you are positioned in relation to your opponent and the best line of attack at that particular moment. Uppercut elbows don't pack that much power because of the short distance you have to gain momentum, but when hitting an opponent on the chin, it often doesn't take much to get a knockout. The technique will leave you well protected against possible attacks, making it a rather safe technique to execute. It is most commonly used in the clinch when two fighters are struggling and swimming for a dominant position. A good uppercut elbow from within the clinch can put distance between you and your opponent, daze your opponent, or open your opponent up for other elbow strikes. It is also commonly employed as a counter against fighters who rush in to break the distance haphazardly. When the two momentums collide, the fight is often over.

Left Uppercut Elbow (Front View)

Chun is demonstrating proper technique for the left uppercut elbow. His left hand is reaching toward the back of his head, casting his left elbow up into his opponent's jaw. His right arm is up, acting as a barrier for counters and protecting the right side of his face. His left shoulder protects his chin. Chun's elbow attack, as shown, is at the end of its course. It's important that it's not thrown any farther because a miss would expose a weakness in your guard. This is enough of an angle to complete an effective attack, yet still leave few openings.

Left Uppercut Elbow (Attack View)

Somphong takes a small step forward and shifts a larger portion of his weight to his lead leg. Once his hips have come forward, he dips them down and then immediately springs them back up using his front leg. Done in one fluid motion, he generates power to rocket his left elbow up into his brother's chin. While executing the technique, his right arm is up protecting his face, and his left shoulder guards his chin. After completing the attack, he uses his left arm to shield his face from a counterattack.

Right Uppercut Elbow (Front View)

Chun is demonstrating proper technique for a right uppercut elbow. His right hand is reaching toward the back of his head, casting his right elbow up into his opponent's jaw. His left arm is up, acting as a barrier for counters and protecting the left side of his face. His right shoulder protects his chin. Chun is also rotating his hips—like throwing a right uppercut punch—to gain power and cover the distance needed to execute his attack. Chun's elbow strike, as shown, is at the end of its course. It is important that it is not thrown any farther because a miss would expose a weakness in your guard. This is enough of an angle to complete an effective attack, yet still leave few openings.

Right Uppercut Elbow (Attack View)

Somphong takes a small step toward Chun, distributes a larger portion of his weight over his lead leg, and turns his hips to his left as if he were executing a right uppercut punch. Once his hips have come forward, they dip down, and then immediately rocket up off his back leg. Done all in one fluid motion, he has covered the distance needed to land his attack and generated power to bring his right elbow straight up into Chun's jaw. During the attack, he keeps his left hand up to protect his face and his chin shielded behind his right shoulder. After completing the attack, he uses his right arm to shield his face from a counterattack.

Diagonal Uppercut Elbow (Front View)

Chun is demonstrating the proper technique for a left diagonal uppercut elbow. His left arm is bent at a forty-five degree angle in relation to the ground, putting the angle halfway between a straight uppercut elbow and a side elbow. His right arm is up, acting as a barrier for counters and protecting the right side of his face. His left shoulder protects his chin. Chun's elbow attack, as shown, is at the end of its course. It's important that you don't throw it any farther because a miss will expose too big an opening. This is just far enough to land your strike and still maintain your guard.

Diagonal Uppercut Elbow (Attack View)

Shifting a larger portion of his weight to his front leg and rotating his hips in a clockwise direction, Somphong performs one fluid motion that involves dipping his hips down and then using his front leg to drive them back up. This movement helps launch his elbow upward at a forty-five degree angle into his brother's chin. During the attack, his right hand protects his face and his left shoulder protects his chin. After the attack, he will use his left arm to further protect his face from a counterattack.

DOWNWARD (JUMPING) ELBOW

The downward elbow is a flashier technique that is usually done by jumping or climbing up your opponent and then bringing the tip of your elbow down onto his head, spine, or collarbone. It is a beautiful technique to see a fighter employ, and when landed cleanly, it can be quite effective. Due to its degree of difficulty, however, it is most commonly seen during Muay Boran (traditional Muay Thai) demonstrations. When executing the technique in actual combat you run the risk of falling over, getting hit with a counter, or missing your target and winding up in a compromising position. It should be done in one fluid motion, climbing up your opponent and then using your downward momentum to land the strike.

Somphong (left) is in a proper Muay Thai stance, searching for an opening on his brother Chun.

Somphong comes forward and places his right foot on top of Chun's left thigh just below his hip, while at the same time reaching his left arm around the back of Chun's head to help him climb up his body. ▶

Propelling himself up using his right leg, Somphong holds onto the back of Chun's head to maintain balance. He places his left foot on top of Chun's right shoulder and raises his right arm in preparation to throw the downward elbow.

Using his weight, Somphong digs the point of his elbow into the top of Chun's head. It is important that your ascent and attack are done in one fluid motion without hesitation. This particular downward elbow is one of the hardest techniques to effectively pull off in Muay Thai competition.

SPINNING BACK ELBOW

The spinning back elbow is another flashy technique. To execute this move you have to spin all the way around, exposing your back and making you vulnerable to counterattacks. If your opponent has his hands up, it is also an easy technique to block. For these reasons, it is best to use as much trickery as possible when performing this move. A good time to pull it off is when you throw a push kick and your opponent blocks it to the outside of his lead leg, causing you to fall forward. This will give you the room and a safe opening to spin around with your elbow. (If you throw a front kick and your opponent sweeps or blocks it to the outside of his lead leg, you will be in the same position.) Once you make contact, it is imperative that you spin back into your stance or pivot around your opponent to avoid leaving yourself open for possible counters. If performed at the right moment with correct technique, the strike can have devastating results. If you manage to knock your opponent out with this strike, you'll probably win a cash prize at the end of the night for the most stylish victory.

Chun (left) is in a proper Muay Thai stance, searching for an opening on his brother Somphong.

Chun starts his attack by stepping to his left foot to the outside of Somphong's lead leg, giving him the proper angle and distance to execute the technique.

Shifting a larger portion of his weight to his left foot, Chun rotates his hips in a clockwise direction and spins on the ball of his left foot. At the same time, he turns his upper body in a clockwise direction, casting his right elbow toward Somphong's face at a diagonal angle. It is important that this technique is executed with speed and precision. Whether you miss or land clean, you should immediately spin back into your stance or pivot around your opponent to avoid any retribution.

BACK UPPERCUT ELBOW

The back uppercut elbow is a rare and flashy technique. Although this strike can certainly knock your opponent out, it is not a common occurrence. Just as with the spinning back

Chun (left) is in a proper Muay Thai stance, searching for an opening on his brother Somphong.

Like the spinning back elbow, Chun starts his attack by stepping his left foot to the outside of his brother's lead leg, giving him the proper distance and angle to execute the technique. Chun's left arm is bent in preparation for the attack, as well as blocking his brother's left arm from punching. His chin is shielded behind his left shoulder to avoid getting hit by a right cross.

Pushing off his left foot, Chun spins his hips and left shoulder in a counterclockwise direction to gain momentum and power for his attack. The tip of his elbow follows a diagonal angle up into Somphong's face. As with the spinning back elbow, it is important that you execute this technique with speed and precision. Whether you land a clean shot or miss, you should immediately step back into your stance or pivot around your opponent to avoid counterattacks.

elbow, the technique exposes your back and opens you up for counters. Nevertheless, it can be an efficient attack when done correctly and at the right moment, pleasing both the judges and fans.

Knees

Like elbow strikes, knees are another Muay Thai trademark, and they are just as feared by fighters. There are three commonly used knee strikes—the straight knee, the side knee, and the jumping side knee—all of which can be targeted at the midsection, head, or legs of your opponent and cause serious damage. Side knees are most effective when thrown from within the clinch, but you must have excellent balance and a good sense of timing to land one amidst all the pushing and pulling. Straight knees can be used while in punching range, usually to counter punches, but they too are most effective when thrown from in the clinch. Because of their degree of difficulty and effectiveness, you should give your knee strikes just as much attention as your kicks. This is especially true if you one day hope to compete in Thailand. Most instructors outside of Thailand shy away from knee and elbow strikes due to the damage they can inflict, and this can give practitioners training under their instruction a false sense of the sport. If you want to learn the true art of Muay Thai, then you must learn how to strike with your knees. The best way to achieve this is to throw thousands of knees on the heavy bag and to practice your knee strikes while clinch sparring. As with all the striking parts of your body, it will take time to develop calluses around your knees. It may be painful at first, but you are almost guaranteed that landing a knee strike will hurt your opponent more. Beating your opponent's midsection with repeated knees can steal his breath and wear him out faster than any other strike.

STRAIGHT KNEE (FRONT AND REAR LEG)

Straight knees are by far the most damaging of the knee strikes, and they can be utilized in a variety of situations. If the time is right, you can simply step forward and throw a straight knee while in punching range, but it's best to set it up using a punch or kick. You can also use it as a counter against an advancing opponent or immediately after you check a Thai kick when in punching range. If throwing it off a check, you're going to step forward with your checking leg before bringing it down to the ground and then immediately follow up with your opposite knee. But like all knee strikes, the straight knee is best used while wrapped up in the clinch because you can pull your opponent into your knee, making the impact even greater. On occasion you'll see a fighter jump in with a straight knee aimed at his opponent's head or midsection, but it's a rare occurrence.

Throwing a straight knee strike with your rear leg packs the most power. If you want to throw a knee with your front leg, you can do so right from your stance, but it most likely won't cause much damage. It is better to first put your front leg into the power position. If you need to cover some distance, this can be achieved by simply stepping forward. If you already have the right distance between you and your opponent, then a switch step will suffice.

Right Straight Knee

Somphong (left) is in a proper Muay Thai stance, searching for an opening on his brother Chun.

Somphong starts his knee strike by bringing his right knee up so that it's level with his hips. Wrapping his right hand around the back of Chun's neck and pulling his brother forward, Somphong comes up onto the ball of his left foot and thrusts his right knee into Chun's midsection. While executing the technique, he keeps his left hand up to protect his face and his right shoulder guarding his chin. It is important that the entire move is done in one fluid motion without hesitation.

Left Straight Knee

Somphong (left) is in a proper Muay Thai stance, searching for an opening on his brother Chun.

Somphong steps forward with his right foot to cover the distance needed to successfully land a left straight knee. If he already had the necessary distance between him and his brother, he would have used a switch step.

Using the forward momentum off the step, Somphong brings his left knee up to waist level, comes up onto the ball of his right foot, traps Chun's left arm with his right hand to stop him from punching, and wraps his left hand around the back of Chun's head. Pulling Chun into the attack, Somphong thrusts his knee into Chun's midsection. It is important that this move is done in one fluid motion—step, knee up, thrust forward.

SIDE KNEE

The side knee is best utilized while fighting for position in the clinch. When done right, it can disrupt your opponent's breathing and score points with the judges. To perform this technique, bring your knee up on the outside of your opponent's body and then drive the side of your knee into his midsection or the side of his thigh. When two good clinchers square off, hundreds of side knees can be thrown in a single bout.

Somphong (left) is tied up with his brother in the clinch, searching for an opening.

To start his attack, Somphong comes up onto the ball of his left foot and raises his right knee to waist level on the outside of Chun's body.

Twisting his hips in a counterclockwise direction, Somphong drives the hard part of his knee into Chun's ribs. He uses his hands, which are wrapped up in the clinch, to maintain balance.

JUMPING SIDE KNEE

The only difference between this technique and the standard side knee is that you're jumping while performing it. It will score more points on the judges' scorecards and produce cheers from the crowd. It's flashy and stylish, but it's also easier for your opponent to throw you to the ground or counter. Therefore, you must make sure your timing is perfect before throwing this technique.

Clinches

The clinch has two different fighting ranges. The first is where you are tied up with your opponent but there is still enough distance between the two of you to throw short-range attacks such as hooks, uppercuts, elbows, and knees. The second range, sometimes referred to as the smother range, is where either one or both of you are locked up in a tight hold, rendering upper-body attacks such as elbows and punches useless, leaving only short-range knees applicable. It is important that you become proficient in both ranges because the clinch is such an essential part of Muay Thai. When wrapped up with your opponent, you have to be sensitive and react to his movements, going more by feel than sight. You have to train your body to pull when your opponent pushes and push when he pulls. One wrong move and you could be on the receiving end of an elbow or a knee. Acquiring the timing and sensitivity needed to be a proficient clinch fighter can take years, but it will be what separates you from kickboxers and karate practitioners. You will be versed and dangerous in a highly ignored range of combat.

Your goal while in the clinch will be to toss your opponent to the ground or pull, push, or throw your opponent off balance so you can land a solid strike. To achieve either you're going to have to learn how to manipulate your opponent's movement so you can achieve a dominant position, such as getting both of your hands wrapped behind your opponent's head. In addition to this, you will also have to develop the endurance it takes to grapple in the clinch, which is vastly different than the endurance needed for fighting in the punching and kicking ranges. In the clinch, your body must stay tight and strong. You're going to want to take quick and steady breaths to ensure that you get enough oxygen to your tightened muscles, as well as always be ready to flex your abdomen and expel your air to protect your organs from hard knee shots.

You should practice the clinch even if you prefer fighting from the outside because there is no telling whom you will be fighting. If you ignore the clinch and your opponent is a clinch master, you're going to be in trouble. Even if you avoid getting knocked out, your opponent will most likely win the decision. Most of the points in a Thai boxing bout are earned in the clinch due to the degree of difficulty of the techniques.

If you are training for a fight, it is best to do at least an hour to an hour and a half of clinch work every day. Some of this time can be spent working technique on the heavy bag, shadowboxing, and on padded rounds with an instructor, but the bulk of your clinch training should come in the form of sparring. This is where you will gain all the attributes needed to be an effective clinch fighter. When sparring in the clinch, however, it is important that you do so in a controlled manner. Use the inside of your thigh when executing side knees and pull your straight knees. If you injure your sparring partner, you will have no one to train with. You are both there to make the other better, not to prove who is more dominant. That comes during a real fight.

THROWS

Throws can be a great way to rack up points on the judges' scorecards, especially if you are locked up in the smother and have no openings to throw a strike. Most throws are executed from a short-range grapple, and because you and your opponent are clinging to one another, usually both of you will go down to the canvas. When this happens, the judges will award points to the fighter who most dominated the toss, which is usually the guy who comes out on top. If neither fighter clearly dominated the toss, then no points will be awarded. You can, however, execute a throw while in the standard clinch by pushing or pulling on your opponent at the right moment, robbing him of balance and sending him crashing down. If you do it correctly, you will be left standing, leaving no doubt in the judges' minds as to who did what.

STANDARD TIE-UP POSITION

In the standard clinch, both fighters have the same tie-up position on the other, creating a neutral position. If two fighters are of equal caliber, this is the position you will most often see in a fight. From here, both combatants will struggle for a more dominant position, such as getting both of their hands behind their opponent's head, which will create an opening for an attack. During the struggle for the dominant position, however, both fighters will still try to throw their opponent, as well as launch attacks and counterattacks. It should be considered a fight within a fight. Your goal is to achieve a dominant position, but while doing so you must also actively throw attacks.

While in the standard tie-up position, you want to remain on the balls of your feet for balance. If you fall back on your heels, you will be easily thrown or countered. You also want to be conscious of where your feet are in relation to your opponent. The goal is to have at least one foot to the outside of your opponent's lead foot. If you don't, it will make it much easier for your opponent to throw you off balance, which in turn will make you vulnerable to attacks. It is important to make sure that your feet are a shoulder's width apart because getting too spread out will put your balance in jeopardy. You also want to keep your body straight and maintain a strong posture, as well as keep your chin down and your shoulders up to protect your face from elbows and make it harder for your opponent to get a firm grip behind your head.

SWIMMING

If your opponent is able to get both hands to the inside position, you could be in trouble if you don't do anything about it. When this happens, you immediately want to fight to get your hands back to the neutral position, which is done by swimming one of your arms through your opponent's grip. If you manage to break your opponent's grip, you will have successfully returned to the neutral tie-up position. The trick is not to allow your opponent to possess a dominant position long enough to unleash an attack. For this reason, the swimming technique should be drilled and redrilled in the gym as much as possible. If you are new to this, you and your training partner should start by switching back and forth between the dominant and standard positions to get a feel for the movement. Once you get it, have your opponent hold onto the dominant position while you attempt to swim through it and break his grip. After you get that down, you can both openly fight for the dominant position. This form of sparring should be including in your daily regimen.

Standard Tie-Up Position (Inside-Inside)

Chun and Somphong are in the standard tie-up position. To achieve this position, Chun slips his right arm to the inside of his brother's left arm. Chun then firmly grips the inside of Somphong's left bicep by hooking his right wrist around it. Chun's left arm is on the outside of Somphong's right arm, and he hooks his left hand around the back of Somphong's head. Chun has his right foot to the outside of Somphong's left foot, but Somphong has his right foot to the outside of Chun's left foot. They each have an equal opportunity to attack the other from this position. To get the upper hand, they will now wrestle for a more dominant position, while at the same time searching for openings to unleash an attack or off-balance their opponent for a throw.

Standard Tie-Up Position (Outside-Outside)

Chun and Somphong are in the second standard tie-up position. To achieve this position, Chun places his right arm on the outside of Somphong's left arm. He then secures the arm by hooking his right wrist over Somphong's bicep. His left arm is on the inside of Somphong's right arm, and his left hand is hooked around the back of his brother's neck. They both have the same hand position, and they both have one foot to the outside of the other's lead leg, giving them both an equal opportunity to attack. To get the upper hand, they will now wrestle for a more dominant position, while at the same time searching for openings to unleash an attack or off-balance their opponent for a throw.

As previously mentioned, from both standard tie-up positions each fighter has an equal opportunity to attack, counter, or throw. Although you may find yourself stuck in this position for some time, you should never remain idle. You should be on a constant quest to get one step ahead of your opponent. The moves you employ to accomplish this, however, will depend entirely upon your opponent's movements. On the quest to gain the upper hand, your opponent is bound to make a mistake because it is very difficult to transition to a more dominant position such as double under-hooks without becoming vulnerable. It is your job to recognize those split seconds where your opponent is weak and capitalize on them. If your opponent makes his move and you miss your window, you should fight to get back into the neutral tie-up position and then work to find the next window. If you're clearly outmatched and want to remain defensive, a good strategy is to mimic the movements of your opponent. If he steps right, you step right. If he pivots, you pivot. Eventually, the referee will break you apart. But instead of assuming a defensive strategy, it is much better to engage in clinch sparring as much as possible during training to hone your skills. This will be the only way for you to get accustomed to the chaotic movements, hand struggles, and constant shifting of positions that accompany every clinch war. It will be the only way to develop your offensive strategy.

PULL-AND-STEP OUT FROM TIE-UP (INSIDE-INSIDE)

This is a maneuver that will leave you in a position where you can knee, elbow, or throw. And if your opponent counters your movement by matching your step, you can easily fall back to the neutral tie-up position. It is common to see two fighters tied up in the clinch perform this maneuver back and forth until one finds an opening.

Pull-and-Step Out to Straight Knee

Chun and Somphong are in the standard tie-up position (inside-inside).

Chun starts his offensive move by stepping to the outside of Somphong's left leg with his right foot. At the same time, he lifts up Somphong's left shoulder and arm with his right arm and pulls down on Somphong's head with his left hand, throwing Somphong off balance.

Continuing to pull down on Somphong's head with his left hand, Chun pivots in a counter-clockwise direction on his right foot, forcing Somphong to step and turn into him. Once he completes his pivot, Chun quickly drives his left knee into Somphong's midsection.

Pull-and-Step Out to Elbow

Chun and Somphong are in the standard tie-up position (inside-inside).

Chun starts by stepping to the outside of Somphong's left leg with his right foot. At the same time, he lifts up Somphong's left shoulder and arm with his right arm and pulls down on Somphong's head with his left hand, throwing Somphong off balance.

Continuing to pull down on Somphong's head with his left hand, Chun takes a small step with his right foot toward the backside of Somphong and then pivots in a counterclockwise direction on his right foot. This forces Somphong to step and turn with him. As Chun completes his pivot, he wastes no time driving an elbow into Somphong's temple.

KICK OUT TO THROW

If your opponent has a strong base, sometimes it can be difficult to pull him off balance by stepping out. When facing such an opponent, shattering his base by kicking out one of his legs is a good technique to employ. If you want to pull your opponent to the left, then you should kick out his left leg. If you want to pull him to the right, then you'll want to kick out his right leg. Timing is imperative with this technique. You must perform the kick and pull at the same time for it to be effective, which can be rather tricky because you're kicking in one direction and pulling in the other. However, when done properly and at the right time, you'll be left in a perfect position to knee your opponent or toss him to the ground.

Chun and Somphong are in the standard tie-up position (inside-inside).

Chun steps to the outside of Somphong's left leg with his right foot. At the same time, he lifts up Somphong's left arm and shoulder with his right arm and pulls Somphong's head down with his left hand, throwing Somphong off balance.

As Chun steps, he feels that Somphong has a strong base. Instead of trying to pivot to Somphong's back, Chun drives his left knee to the inside of Somphong's inner left thigh, disrupting Somphong's balance.

With his left hand firmly gripped around the back of Somphong's head, Chun turns his upper body in a counterclockwise direction, pulling Somphong's head along. At the same time, he lifts Somphong's left leg with his left knee and turns his hips in a clockwise direction. The two actions sweep Somphong off his feet.

BASIC DEFENSE (GETTING THE HAND OFF THE BACK OF YOUR HEAD)

In order to transition from the neutral tie-up to a more dominant position, you must first learn how to get your opponent's hand off the back of your head. If your opponent controls your head, even if it is only partially controlled with one arm, he can manipulate and tweak your movements. In most cases, both fighters will attempt to strip their opponent's hand from their head. The first fighter to achieve this goal will suddenly have a lot more options open up. He can quickly snatch a more dominant lock or perform any number of strikes or throws. The trick is to achieve this before your opponent does. If you manage this, you should capitalize on the opening immediately because your opponent's new goal will be to reacquire the standard tie-up position.

Somphong has managed to reach up and grip the back of Chun's head with his inside arm, putting both of his arms on the inside of Chun's arms.

Knowing he is in a vulnerable position, Chun moves quickly to get Somphong's hand off the back of his head. He does this by turning his right shoulder in a clockwise direction, pressing his shoulder up toward his chin, and turning his head slightly away from Somphong's grip.

Rotating his right shoulder all the way over, Chun turns his hips away from Somphong to break the grip and clear his brother's arm. At the same time, Chun keeps Somphong's left arm trapped with his right hand. This will prevent Somphong from reaching his left hand around the right side of Chun's head. Now that the hold is broken, Chun has several options. He can step back into punching range, pivot out and try to take Somphong's back, or return to the clinch fight.

PUSH-AND-STEP OUT

This is another technique that two fighters often employ from the standard tie-up because if done successfully, it leaves you in a position to knee, elbow, or throw. It works well in conjunction with the pull-and-step, where you step out and pull your opponent off balance just enough for you to step out to the opposite side and push him farther off balance, allowing you to land a number of attacks. Fighters will often go back and forth, pulling and pushing, until an opening presents itself or their opponent makes a mistake.

Push-and-Step Out to Straight Knee

Chun and Somphong are in the standard tie-up position.

In order to step to the outside of Somphong and take control of the clinch battle, Chun first needs to get his brother's right hand off the back of his head. If he tries to step out without getting rid of the hand, Somphong can hinder his movements by providing resistance on his head. To accomplish his mission, Chun presses his left shoulder up toward his chin, turns his head slightly away from his brother, and rotates his hips in a clockwise direction. At the same time, he traps Somphong's left arm using his right hand. This will not only keep Somphong from wrapping his left hand around the back of Chun's head, but Chun can also use his control of Somphong's arm to help steer his brother's movements. Having good technique, Chun collapses Somphong's grip using the turn of his body and his left shoulder.

Immediately after breaking Somphong's hold, Chun steps to the outside of his brother's right foot with his left foot. Pivoting in a clockwise direction on his left foot, Chun pushes down on Somphong's head with both hands to cause his brother's weight to fall forward.

Seeing his opening, Chun delivers a straight right knee to Somphong's solar plexus.

Push-and-Step Out to Elbow

Chun and Somphong are in the standard tie-up position.

In order to step to the outside of Somphong and take control of the clinch battle, Chun first needs to get his brother's right hand off the back of his head. If he tries to step out without getting rid of the hand, Somphong can hinder his movements by providing resistance on his head. To accomplish his mission, Chun presses his left shoulder up toward his chin, rotates his hips in a clockwise direction, and turns his head slightly away from Somphong's grip. At the same time, he traps Somphong's left arm using his right hand. This will not only keep Somphong from wrapping his left hand around the back of Chun's head, but Chun can also use his control of Somphong's arm to help steer his brother's movements. Having good technique, Chun collapses Somphong's grip using the turn of his body and his left shoulder.

Immediately after breaking Somphong's hold, Chun steps to the outside of his brother's right foot with his left foot. Pivoting in a clockwise direction on his left foot, Chun pushes down on Somphong's head with his left hand to cause his brother's weight to fall forward.

Still maintaining control of Somphong's head with his left hand, Chun takes advantage of the opening by stepping forward and delivering a right uppercut elbow to Somphong's temple.

DOMINANT CLINCH POSITION (BOTH HANDS BEHIND THE HEAD)

If you are able to swim your hands to the inside of your opponent's arms, then you have reached a dominant position from which you can easily maneuver your opponent and throw him off balance, giving you numerous options. Close-range elbow strikes work wonderfully because both of your hands/arms are on the inside of your opponent's arms, leaving no blockade between your weapon and his face. Now that you control his head, you also control his body, which opens up knee strikes as well. Pushing him off balance will create an opening to land a hard knee to his midsection or face. But before attempting knee attacks, you will want to secure your hold by locking your hands together behind your opponent's head. This can be done a couple of different ways. The first is with the hand clasp, in which the top of one hand is resting on the palm of the other. Both hands are open and pressed tightly against the back of your opponent's skull. The other is the fighter's hand lock, where each palm is cupping the other, tightly locked together. Once you have picked one of the holds, you want to maintain a strong grip. This can be achieved by squeezing your elbows together, pinching your opponent's head. If your opponent has a strong neck and you're having trouble pulling his head down, try digging your elbows into his collarbones, causing him to buckle under the pain. It's important that you don't try to muscle your opponent's head down. You want to use the weight of your body to pull it down. Stepping back and dropping your hips can accomplish this. Once in this glorious position, you can either step and pivot out or deliver a straight knee.

Double Hands Behind the Head to Straight Knee

Chun and Somphong are in the standard tie-up position (outside-inside).

Chun removes his right hand from Somphong's bicep, moves it underneath his brother's left arm, and then slips it up through the narrow gap between Somphong's head and left arm. Forcing it through this gap, Chun reaches his right hand around the back of Somphong's head.

To secure his dominant hold, Chun grips both hands high up on the back of his brother's head and squeezes his elbows together.

Keeping his hold tight, Chun steps back with his right foot, drops his hips, and presses his weight down on top of his brother. This forces Somphong's head toward the ground and sets Chun up for a knee strike.

Coming up onto the ball of his left foot, Chun thrusts his hips up and forward, driving his knee into Somphong's solar plexus. To ensure his brother takes the full impact of the knee, Chun continues to force Somphong's head down with his hands.

Optional Holds: Hand Clasp and Hand Lock

Chun is using a hand clasp to grip Somphong's head. His right hand is on top of his left, palm to knuckles. His elbows are pinched tightly together to maintain control of his brother's head and cut off the blood supply to his brain.

Chun is using a hand lock to grip Somphong's head. His left palm is facing up and his right palm is facing down. To get the most out of his grip, he wraps the fingers of each hand around the top of the other hand. His elbows are pinched tightly together to maintain control of his brother's head and cut off the blood supply to his brain.

Double Hands Behind the Head to Side Knee

Chun has secured a dominant clinch position by getting both of his arms to the inside of Somphong's arms. He secures the hold by clasping his hands together, pinching Somphong's head with his elbows, and forcing his brother's head down.

Maintaining a strong grip around Somphong's head and coming up onto the ball of his left foot, Chun lifts his right knee on the outside of his brother's body. He lifts his knee to the height of his target, which in this case happens to be his brother's ribs.

Maintaining a strong hold on Somphong's head, Chun rotates his hips in a counterclockwise direction, slamming the inside of his right knee into Somphong's ribs. He maintains control of his brother's body after impact by keeping his hold tight.

Double Hands Behind the Head to Step-and-Turn Out to Knee

Chun has secured a dominant clinch position by getting both of his arms to the inside of Somphong's arms. He secures the hold by clasping his hands together, pinching his elbows toward each other, and forcing his brother's head down.

Chun steps to the outside of Somphong's right leg with his left foot. He then pivots on his left foot, using his hips, the weight of his body, and the strength in his arms to pull Somphong forward and throw him off balance.

Pulling Somphong's head forward and down with his hands, Chun comes up onto the ball of his left foot, thrusts his hips up and forward, and drives his right knee into Somphong's solar plexus.

BREAKING DOUBLE HANDS BEHIND HEAD TO KNEE

If your opponent manages to get both hands behind your head, you should quickly work to return to the neutral tie-up position, lock him up with the double under-hooks, or get his hands off the back of your head before he can land an attack and cause damage. The last of these options tends to have the best results. This is achieved by pushing off your opponent's face with both hands to create distance and break his hold.

Chun has secured a dominant clinch position by getting both of his arms to the inside of Somphong's arms. He secures the hold by clasping his hands together, pinching his elbows toward each other, and forcing his brother's head down.

Knowing he is in a vulnerable position, Somphong places both hands on Chun's face and pushes away. At the same time, he steps back with his left leg. The combined movements create distance and break Chun's hold. It is important to note that Somphong is not dropping his head when executing this technique. He uses the muscles in his neck to keep his head upright so his brother can't land a knee to his face.

Taking advantage of the separation, Somphong drives a straight left knee into Chun's solar plexus.

OVER-UNDER TO BACK TO SIDE KNEE

This is a difficult maneuver to pull off, but if executed at the right moment, it will leave you in a position to do serious damage to your opponent. It is similar to the pull-and-step out maneuver, except with this technique you're lifting up on your opponent's arm and stepping through. Once you reach your opponent's back, it is imperative that you quickly secure and tighten the lock because your opponent will feel your actions and immediately try to scramble away. Usually when you see this move in a match, one fighter is trying to secure his opponent's back and land his attacks while the other fighter is desperately trying to escape, causing the two fighters to run circles around each other in the ring. But if you can secure the lock tight, you will be free to drive the side of your knee into your opponent's back or land short knees to his thigh. The lock itself is also dangerous. When squeezed tightly enough, your opponent's shoulder will dig into one side of his neck and your arm will dig into the other side of his neck, cutting off the blood flow to his brain. Usually you won't have enough time to choke him unconscious because the ref will intervene. For this reason, it is important to land as many attacks as possible and rack up points before the ref breaks you apart.

Chun and Somphong are in the standard tie-up position (inside-inside).

Chun steps to the outside of Somphong's left leg with his right foot. At the same time, he lifts up with his right arm to raise Somphong's left arm and shoulder. This allows him to move underneath his brother's arm and get to his back.

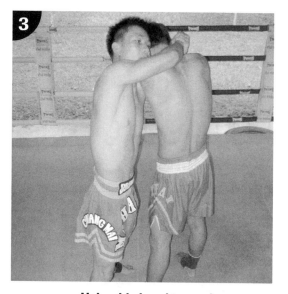

Using his head to apply pressure to the back of Somphong's left arm, Chun reaches around Somphong's back with his right arm and locks his palms together. To secure a tight lock, Chun pulls his hands into his body while driving his left shoulder up into his brother.

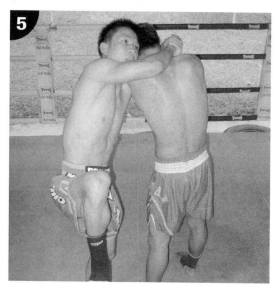

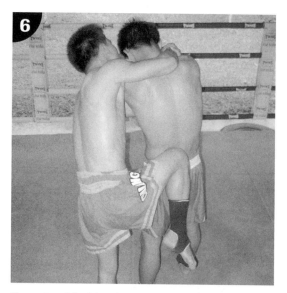

Maintaining a strong grip around Somphong's head, Chun comes up onto the ball of his left foot and brings his right knee up on the outside of his brother's body.

Rotating his hips in a counterclockwise direction, Chun drives the inside of his right knee into Somphong's back. As he does this, he keeps a tight hold to maintain control of Somphong's body after impact.

DOUBLE UNDER-HOOKS

The double under-hook position is where both of your arms are under your opponent's arms and your hands are locked together behind his back. Although this is a dominant position, you must hold the lock tight so your opponent can't break your grip and grab the back of your head with both of his hands, thereby giving him the dominant position. Landing elbow strikes from the double under-hook position will be impossible, but you will be well protected against your opponent's elbow and knee strikes. To land a knee strike from this position, you'll first have to step back and create the needed distance, while at the same time holding the lock tight. This can be achieved by dropping your weight and hips down for balance and control. Throwing your opponent, however, will be much easier because you have the needed leverage and control over his upper body.

Double Under-Hooks to Lift-and-Sweep

Chun and Somphong are in the standard tie-up position (inside-inside).

Somphong releases his grip from around Chun's arm and head. To establish the double under-hook lock, he drops his weight down while moving his arms underneath Chun's arms. Clasping his hands together, he squeezes his hands toward his body to lock his brother in tight.

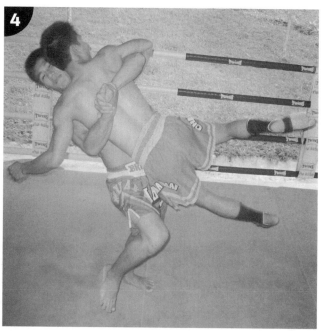

Somphong lifts Chun by pushing off the ground with his legs, squeezing his arms in tightly, and thrusting his hips forward. Once Chun's feet are off the ground, Somphong does three things in one fluid motion to execute the throw. He turns his upper body to his right, rotates his hips to his left, and uses his right knee to sweep his brother's legs out from underneath him.

Double Under-Hooks to Step-and-Sweep

Chun has established the double under-hook lock on Somphong.

To throw Somphong off balance, Chun squeezes the lock tight by sucking his hands in toward his stomach and pushing his shoulders into Somphong's upper body.

Chun places his right foot on the outside of Somphong's left foot. To throw his brother farther off balance and set him up for the trip, Chun shifts the majority of his weight to his right foot and drives his upper body forward. To trip his brother over his leg, Chun turns his hips and upper body in a clockwise direction.

BREAKING DOUBLE UNDER-HOOKS
TO STRAIGHT KNEE

The best defense for double under-hooks is to avoid getting caught in the position altogether. When your opponent drops his weight down to wrap both hands behind your back, you can counter by stepping back and creating more distance. Your opponent will most likely drive forward in an attempt to break the distance, but you can stop his forward progression by driving your elbows down into his collarbones. If, however, your opponent comes in too quickly and you find yourself stuck in this lock, it is important that you immediately drop your weight and put as much distance between your hips and your opponent's hips as possible. Also, wrap your hands over your opponent's arms and push away from his body. Your opponent's offense will depend heavily on getting your upper body straight so he can control your hips, making it extremely easy for him to execute a throw.

Somphong has secured the double under-hooks on his brother. Knowing he is in a bad position, Chun drops his weight and uses his hands to push off his brother's body, creating separation between their hips.

Taking a step back with his right foot and driving his weight backward, Chun squeezes his elbows tightly together to break his brother's lock. He maintains a low stance and uses his hands to keep separation between their hips. Having successfully broken the lock and created distance between him and his brother, Chun has the ability to pivot out and execute a throw, continue to fight from in the clinch, or execute a straight knee strike to his brother's midsection.

Using the separation he created and Somphong's forward momentum, Chun drives his right knee into his brother's stomach. To get the most out of the strike, he uses his arms, which are still to the outside of his brother's arms, to pull Somphong's body into the attack. Immediately after his blow has landed, Chun will step his right foot back and drive his weight down onto his brother to ensure that Somphong doesn't reacquire the double under-hook lock.

BREAKING DOUBLE UNDER-HOOKS WITH LEG

Many times when an opponent has you trapped in a double under-hook lock, you will be able to create space by sitting your hips back but still not be able to break the hold. In such cases, this technique comes in handy.

1 Chun has secured the double under-hooks on his brother.

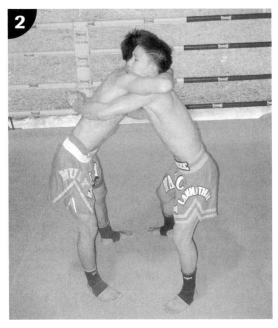

2 Knowing he is in a bad position, Somphong drops his weight back to create separation between his hips and his brother's hips.

3 Unable to break his brother's lock, Somphong throws his right leg across his brother's hips to maintain the separation.

4 Driving his leg into Chun's hips and pulling his upper body back, Somphong breaks Chun's hold and throws him off balance, putting him in a good position to attack.

Breaking Double Under-Hooks with Leg (Variation)

Chun has secured the double under-hooks on his brother.

Knowing he is in a bad position, Somphong drops his weight back to create separation between his hips and his brother's hips.

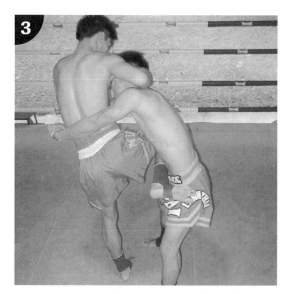

This time he places his right knee against his brother's right hip, which turns his body in a counterclockwise direction.

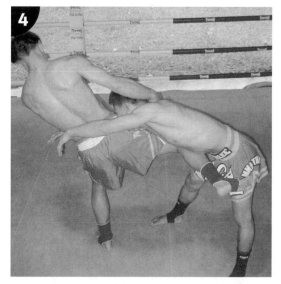

Driving his leg into Chun's hips and pulling his upper body back, Somphong breaks Chun's hold and throws him off balance, putting him in a good position to attack.

DEFENSE AND COUNTERS

Basic Defense

In Muay Thai, it's always better to be the one attacking than the one being attacked. However, you can't throw strikes at your opponent without your opponent throwing something back, which is why you must know how to block every strike that can be unleashed. Having a good defensive game will never win you a fight, but it can save you from getting knocked out or losing points on the judges' scorecards. It will also eliminate your fear of your opponent countering one of your attacks, making you more aggressive.

Ideally, the best defense is to simply get out of the way of an attack, but sometimes you'll have to put up a block because your opponent counters while you're in mid attack or you simply don't have enough time to move out of a strike's path. You can block using your shin, knee, arms, elbows, hands, and in some situations your head. Blocking does hurt because you're still taking the impact of the blow, but when done correctly, it should hurt a lot less than if you didn't put up a block. Once you execute a block, you're going to want to return to your fighting stance or launch an attack of your own. Launching your own attack should be done as often as possible because your opponent will be out of position from his attack, presenting you with an opportunity to do some damage. Most times, fighters throw the exact same attack that was thrown at them. For example, when you check a low kick aimed at your lead leg, immediately after the check, throw a low kick aimed at your opponent's lead leg. If you are fast enough, your opponent won't have time to bring his kicking leg back and put up a check of his own.

Defensive Techniques

CHECKING (BLOCKING) KICKS

Learning how to check or block kicks is mandatory in Muay Thai. Some martial arts require that you swivel your arm down to block a kick, but in Thai boxing that will usually result in a broken arm or a shin to the side of your unprotected face. Instead, you want to create a solid barrier on whichever side of your body the kick is aimed at. If your opponent throws a Thai kick at your ribs on the left side of your body, you check the kick by lifting your left leg so your knee comes to the inside of your left elbow. With your leg covering the lower half of your body and your arm covering the upper half of your body, you now have a solid barrier between your vulnerable areas and the kick. There is, however, a lot of varying opinions on proper form. Some believe you should come up onto the ball of your planted foot, while others think you should remain flat-footed. Some believe you should point the toes of your raised foot down, while others believe you should point the toes of your raised foot at your opponent. Some believe you should lower your arm to meet your leg, and others believe you should raise your leg to meet your arm. It's all a matter of preference.

Whatever way you decide to check, the only thing that truly matters is that your technique can efficiently block a kick and leave you balanced to fire off an attack of your own. In order to achieve that, your check must adhere to a few universal rules. You want to block a Thai kick aimed at your ribs with the middle of your shin. This requires that your leg is raised to the correct height, as well as angled at a forty-five degree angle in relation to your opponent. If your knee is pointed straight at your opponent, he will end up kicking your thigh. If your leg is angled too far away from your opponent, you run the risk of the kick slipping by your guard and hitting its target. You also want to distribute your weight to the leg still planted on the ground. This will help keep you grounded and prevent a kick from penetrating your guard and knocking you to the canvas. Your planted leg should tighten upon impact, but you don't want to drive your weight into the kick because that will most often cause you to fall forward after you have checked. You don't want to fall forward; you want to immediately return to your normal stance or launch a counterattack.

Depending on your position, at times you may want to execute a cross-check instead of the traditional check. This is achieved by bringing your leg across your body to block a kick coming at the opposite side. Either way, expect a fair amount of pain in the beginning. It takes a lot of time to callus your shins to block hard kicks.

CHECKING LOW THAI KICK WITH FRONT LEG

Blocking low kicks is relatively simple. All you have to do is lift the leg being targeted and angle it so that the kick collides with your knee. However, low kicks can pack a lot of power, and blocking this kick can hurt you as well as your opponent. If you are able, it is best to counter this kick with a push kick or by stepping back and out of the way (see Counters section). Some fighters also counter low kicks with straight punches, especially against opponents who tend to drop their hands when they kick. If you land the punch before the kick impacts, which is possible because a straight punch is faster than a circular kick, then you will take a significant amount of the kick's momentum away. However, you can't always rely on being so speedy with a counter. When in doubt, it is best to block the kick. If the kick is aimed low, it is important not to raise your leg too high. If you do this more than one time in a fight, your opponent will probably start throwing his low kicks underneath your checking leg and targeting your rear calf muscle. It is important to gauge the destination of the kick, a skill that can be earned through hours of sparring. If you gauge right and block a low kick with your knee rather than your shin, the solid barrier will send a painful shock wave up your opponent's leg, making him think twice about throwing another hard low kick.

CHECKING MID-RANGE THAI KICK WITH FRONT LEG

Stepping out of the way of a Thai kick aimed at your midsection is a little trickier, and it usually requires that you step back and

Somphong blocks a right low kick by bringing his left leg up at a forty-five degree angle to his brother, ensuring that Chun's shin will collide with his knee. It is important when executing this check that your foot doesn't come too high. If you raise your leg to the same height as you would when blocking a rib kick, there is a good chance that your opponent will throw his kick beneath your check and target your rear calf muscle.

lean back at the same time. Checking this kick is also more difficult. While on one leg, you're trying to stop a very powerful kick. However, this check absolutely must be learned because of the amazing number of kicks aimed at the midsection during the course of a fight. It is simply impossible to get out of the way of all of them. Like most techniques, there are varying views on proper technique. The technique shown in the photo is the most common. (When an opponent kicks to your rear leg, the same block can be executed with your opposite leg.)

It is important to keep your mind open and always try new ways of executing the same technique because it's impossible to know what works best for you until you try everything. Muay Thai fighters are constantly refining their game; it's a part of what makes it such an effective style. Unlike karate and tae kwon do practitioners, no two Thai boxers fight exactly the same.

Chun blocks Somphong's kick by bringing his left knee up to the inside of his left elbow, forming a solid barrier on the left side of his body. To ensure that Somphong's kick doesn't sneak around his barrier, Chun has lifted his leg at a forty-five degree angle to his brother. He keeps his grounded leg tense so he can absorb the impact of the kick without falling back, and his right hand is thrust out to gauge distance. Once he has completed the block, Chun will either return to his normal fighting stance or move in for his own attack.

CROSS-CHECK

When two fighters are well versed in Muay Thai, it can be a difficult task to land a clean blow. If you throw up a check every time your opponent throws a kick, the chances are he will start throwing fake strikes to catch you off guard. For example, your opponent might fake a right kick to your front leg, which causes you to raise your front leg to check the kick. While your leg is off the ground, he switches to a left kick to your rear leg. Your goal should be to quickly move out of the way or check the kick with your rear leg, but sometimes you just won't have enough time. In such a case, you can perform a cross-check, which is where you bring your lead leg across your body and block the kick aimed at your rear leg or ribs. The same rules apply to this check as the standard one. You want to form a solid barrier with your leg and arm, except in this case you will be using a leg from one side and an arm from the other. You want to tighten up your grounded leg and keep your posture strong so the impact doesn't knock you off balance. Then immediately after the check you want to return to your stance or execute a counterattack.

Somphong blocks Chun's left Thai kick by bringing his left leg across his body to the inside of his right arm, forming a solid barrier on the right side of his body. He leans slightly into the kick to keep himself from getting knocked off balance, and he keeps his hands up for defense. Once the block is complete, Somphong will either return to his normal fighting stance or launch an attack.

BLOCKING THE HEAD KICK

If you're not certain if your opponent's kick is headed for your ribs or head, it is best to throw up the standard block to be on the safe side. Just make sure that your arm is up high enough to provide adequate protection for your head. However, if you are certain the kick is aimed high, covering your head with your arms will do. You want to make sure that your arm is pressed snugly against your head or you risk absorbing the entire impact with your arm and possibly breaking it in the process.

Chun blocks Somphong's head kick by reaching his right hand to the back of his head and placing the bulk of his arm snugly against the side of his head. He turns slightly away from the kick so that the blow is taken by his arm and shoulder. He remains strong and tight to ensure the kick doesn't sneak through his barrier or knock his arm into his jaw.

BLOCKING WITH YOUR ARMS

If you get into the habit of dropping your hands while training in the gym, the chances are that the bad habit will carry over into the ring. Your head is the most important part of your body to protect, and keeping your hands up is the best way to protect it. In Muay Thai, you want to keep your hands up at eye level so you can quickly block kicks, punches, or elbows that come your way. It is important that your arms stay close to your head. If you stick them out at a ninety-degree angle to block a head kick, your arm will probably get broken. In addition, circular strikes such as hooks and head kicks will most likely wrap around your extended arm and still make contact with your head. For these reasons, it is better to block circular attacks by bringing your arm up and placing it snugly against the side of your face and head. It's still going to be jarring, but if you lean slightly away from the attack, it will lessen the blow. If the attack is coming straight in, it's best to bring your arms in tight, covering your head. It is important when doing this, however, not to bring your arms so tight together that they block your vision. If you blind yourself, you won't be able to see what is coming next or be able to find an opening to throw a counterattack. Elbows can also be used to block, directing them toward the attack and causing your opponent a serious amount of pain. If his punch or leg hits your elbow flush, there is a good chance he will break or fracture his hand or shin. And as with all techniques, every block begins and ends in your proper stance.

Blocking the Hook

Chun demonstrates the proper technique for blocking a left hook to the head. He reaches his right hand toward the back of his head and places the bulk of his arm snugly against the side of his head. Although he turns slightly away to absorb the majority of the impact with his arm and shoulder, he keeps his eyes forward, locked on his opponent.

Blocking the Uppercut

Chun demonstrates the proper technique for blocking an uppercut. He reaches his right arm across his face so the punch will be blocked with his elbow, leaving no room for the punch to sneak through. He extends his left arm to gauge his distance from his opponent.

Blocking Straight Punches

Chun demonstrates the proper technique to block a straight punch. He brings both of his hands close to the sides of his head, keeping them tight. He angles his head down so the top of his head will block any punches that may slip through the gap between his arms or punches that are thrown from over the top, such as the overhand right. However, the aim with this technique is to block with the tip of your elbow, causing your opponent damage.

PUSH BLOCK

If you are close to your opponent and can see his kick or knee coming, sometimes you can block his attack with a simple push. This technique comes in very handy when you don't have the time to lift your leg and check. Timing is critical. The idea is to catch your opponent midway through his attack with your closer arm. He will be on one leg, and it won't take much to throw him off balance and rob the momentum from his attack. This will also put you in a good position to throw a counterattack. To get the most out of this technique, you should push off your opponent's chest, keep your other hand up to protect your face, and tuck your chin behind your shoulder.

Although the push block shown in the photo is for a straight knee attack, you can also perform it against a kick, when your opponent blocks one of your attacks (see Chapter 5), or even off one of your own attacks, such as throwing a punch and then pushing your opponent off balance as he attempts to block the punch.

Push Block for a Knee Strike

Thrusting his left arm forward and pushing off Somphong's chest, Chun stops his brother's forward momentum and the straight knee attack. While executing the block, Chun has his chin tucked behind his left shoulder and his right hand up to protect his face.

BODY CHECK

A body check is where you place one of your legs across your opponent's hips to block a knee or kick, or to create distance between you and your opponent. This technique often comes in handy when you throw a Thai kick or side knee and your opponent steps toward you. Not wanting him to be able to tie you up in the clinch while you're on one foot, you slide your leg across his hips to block his attack. It also works well in the clinch. If you can wedge your leg across your opponent's hips while tied up, you can create distance by pushing him away with your leg. It is important that you remain in this position just long enough to push off and then immediately return to your normal fighting stance. If your opponent grabs your leg and steps back, you'll be thrown off balance. If you feel this happening, forcefully push off him to regain control of your leg.

This move works very well when your Thai kick slips past your opponent's ribs and across his hips. With most fighters trained to immediately launch a counterattack, this technique will keep your opponent at bay long enough for you to return to your normal fighting stance.

Seeing his brother move forward and sensing he will attack, Somphong places his left leg across Chun's hips to stop his forward momentum and any attack he might launch. He drives his weight down into Chun's hips to force him backward and then pushes off Chun's hips to give him the momentum to return to his normal fighting stance.

Countering Kicks

When your opponent attacks, countering is by far your best method of defense. The idea is to intercept your opponent's attack by either getting out of the way, blocking, throwing, or catching, and then deal an attack of your own before he can return all of his limbs back to their proper place in his stance. For every attack thrown there are numerous counters, and deciding which one to pick depends on what your opponent throws, how he throws it, and where he aims. Getting out of the way is the best option because when you make your opponent miss, it almost always leaves an opening that you can take advantage of.

A lot of fighters base the majority of their game on counterattacking. They sit back and play their cards coolly, but the moment their opponent comes in with an attack, they get out of the way and then unleash. If you find yourself in the ring with such an opponent, it can be very frustrating because every time you come in to attack, you end up suffering. Basing your entire game off countering, however, will probably not win you many fights. The judges and fans like to see offensive and aggressive fighters, so you don't want to be looking for a counter so much as be ready to deliver one. Whatever techniques your opponent employs, be alert and ready to send a painful rebuttal.

STEPPING OUT OF THE WAY

For most low kicks, merely stepping out of the way and making your opponent miss will give you an opening to attack. Those openings usually don't last very long, so to capitalize on them you must have good timing and judgment. First you must be able to spot the opening, then know what attacks will be able to slip through that opening, and finally you must have the coordination and quickness to launch your attack without hesitation. If you miss your window, your opponent will either launch another attack or return to his normal stance.

Countering Low Thai Kick with Step Back to Kick

Somphong (right) is in a proper Muay Thai stance, searching for an opening on Chun.

Chun steps in to throw a low kick to the inside of Somphong's lead leg.

Just as Chun's kick is about to make contact, Somphong steps back with his left foot, putting him into a right lead stance (southpaw). Missing the kick, Chun's momentum carries him around and presents Somphong with an opening for a counterattack.

Taking advantage of the opening, Somphong fires a left Thai kick to Chun's chin. It is important that this technique is done fast. If you hesitate, your opponent will reacquire his normal fighting stance and your window of opportunity to land a clean counterattack will have closed.

Countering Low Thai Kick with Step Back to Kick (Variation)

Somphong (left) is in a proper Muay Thai stance, searching for an opening on Chun.

Chun throws a right Thai kick to Somphong's lead leg.

Just as Chun's kick is about to make contact with its target, Somphong steps back with his left foot into a right lead stance (southpaw), avoiding the attack. Missing the kick, Chun's momentum carries him around and presents Somphong with an opening for a counterattack.

Taking advantage of the opening, Somphong throws a left Thai kick to the back of Chun's head. It is important that this technique is done fast. If you hesitate, your opponent will reacquire his normal fighting stance and your window of opportunity to land a clean counterattack will have closed.

COUNTERING PUSH KICKS

Trying to block a push kick isn't the best approach. They are usually thrown to create separation, and if you block the kick with an arm or a leg, your body will still absorb the impact and get pushed away. One of the best options is to catch your opponent's push kick. Once you have control of his leg, you can use it to manipulate his entire body and create openings for a punch, elbow, kick, knee, or sweep. You can even hold on to his leg and attack him while he's balancing on one foot. If you have control of his leg, the counterattacks are numerous.

Catching a push kick is not as simple as it appears, especially if you're fighting a seasoned veteran. The first thing you want to do when executing this technique is pivot out of the way of the kick. Deciding which side to pivot to depends upon which leg your opponent uses to kick. If he kicks with his right leg, you should pivot on your left foot, putting you on the outside of his body. If your opponent kicks with his left leg, you want to pivot on your right foot, once again putting you on the outside of his body. This will ensure that you're not left standing right in front of your opponent where he can follow up with other strikes.

Next, you have to either gain control of his leg or redirect his kick. If your intent is to hold on to your opponent's kick and land strikes while he's on one foot, you should grab around his ankle with one hand and pull upward to throw him off balance. It is important to use a firm grip because when trapped in this compromising position your opponent will apply downward pressure to his leg or try to jump into you in an effort to free himself. If your goal is to redirect the kick, you'll want to scoop his foot more than grab it, and then fling it to whichever side will expose his back. This scoop is usually done with your hand, but it can also be done with your leg. When you see a fighter use his leg to redirect a push kick, most of the time it's because he brought his leg up thinking his opponent was going to throw a Thai kick. Instead of dropping his leg back down and trying to redirect the push kick using his hand, he simply brings his leg across the front of the opponent's body like a cross-check, redirecting the push kick just like he would have if he'd used his hand.

Counter Rear Push Kick to Kick

Chun (left) is in a proper Muay Thai stance, searching for an opening on his brother Somphong.

Somphong brings his right knee up in preparation to throw a push kick.

To avoid getting hit with the attack, Chun pivots in a clockwise direction on the ball of his left foot. At the same time, he catches Somphong's right ankle with his left hand, wrapping his fingers around his brother's Achilles tendon for a tight hold.

To expose Somphong's back and create an opening, Chun throws his brother's leg away from his body.

Chun immediately takes advantage of the opening and fires a right Thai kick to Somphong's ribs.

Counter Front Push Kick to Sweep

Chun (left) is in a proper Muay Thai stance, searching for an opening on his brother.

Somphong brings his left knee up in preparation to throw a push kick.

3

4

Somphong extends his left leg for the kick, and Chun reacts by stepping back, putting him out of the kick's range. He catches Somphong's ankle with his left hand, wrapping his fingers around his Achilles tendon for a tight grip.

Chun maneuvers Somphong's foot to his left side. This exposes Somphong's back, as well as gives Chun room to step forward and cover the distance needed to execute a sweep.

5

6

Maintaining a firm grip on Somphong's ankle with his left hand, Chun unleashes a right low kick to Somphong's right calf and pushes Somphong's upper body in the opposite direction of the kick using his right arm. If done with enough power, you can dump your opponent on his head rather than his back.

Counter Rear Push Kick with Cross-Check to Knee

Chun (left) is in a proper Muay Thai stance, searching for an opening on his brother.

Somphong brings his right knee up in preparation to throw a right push kick.

To intercept Somphong's kick, Chun brings his left knee up. In order to redirect the attack and cause Somphong's momentum to carry him forward, Chun catches the kick with his shin and pushes it to his right side using his leg. This movement is similar to performing a cross-check.

Having guided the kick to his right side, forcing his brother to fall into a southpaw stance and expose his back, Chun immediately places his left foot behind Somphong. He is now in a perfect position to launch a counterattack.

164

Before Somphong has a chance to return to his normal fighting stance, Chun takes advantage of the opening and fires a knee into his brother's stomach.

COUNTER REAR THAI KICK WITH LEAN BACK TO REAR THAI KICK

When an opponent throws a punch or kick at your body or head, the best method of defense is to get out of the way of the attack and make your opponent miss. And one of the easiest ways to make your opponent miss is to simply lean back. It can be done against a punch or kick aimed at your body or head, and the technique is rather simple. Taking a step back, you want to bend your rear leg and place your weight down on top of it. While leaning back on your hips, keep your rear hand up to protect your face and drop your front hand so the kick can go whirling by. Once this happens, you want to immediately bring your weight back forward and launch a counterattack before your opponent can reposition himself in his stance.

Timing and sense of distance are crucial. If you misread the kick in any way or your reactions are too slow, your opponent will land a clean kick that could have devastating results. But if your timing is on and you immediately follow the lean back with a counterattack, lashing out with it like a cobra, you will have gained the admiration of the crowd for executing a beautiful technique and scored points on the judges' scorecards. You will also have taught your opponent a lesson, making him think twice before charging in with another attack.

Chun (left) is in a proper Muay Thai stance, searching for an opening on his brother.

Somphong throws a right Thai kick at Chun's head. Reacting quickly, Chun steps back with his right foot and leans back at the waist, maintaining balance by keeping his back leg slightly bent. Chun keeps his right hand up to protect his face, but he drops his left hand to make way for the kick. He doesn't want anything to stop the kick's momentum, which will carry his brother's body around and expose his back, creating an opening in the process.

The momentum of the kick is too much to stop, and Somphong exposes his back as he brings his right leg to the ground. Chun takes advantage of the opening by springing forward and firing a right Thai kick to Somphong's ribs.

CATCHING THAI KICKS

Catching an opponent's Thai kick aimed at your ribs or head is a good way to throw him off balance and create openings for an attack of your own. Checking Thai kicks is a whole lot safer, but sometimes you won't be in a position to throw up a check. And sometimes you'll want to make your opponent pay for attacking you. Your first movement when executing this technique should be to take a step away from the kick so you don't absorb the full brunt of the impact. It will still hurt, but it will hurt a lot less than if you didn't move. Next, you need to either catch the kick or redirect it.

To catch a kick, you want to trap your opponent's leg between your ribs and arm. Your opponent will quickly realize what has happened and apply downward pressure to his leg in an attempt to free it. To hinder his escape, wrap your hand around his ankle and then crank his leg up into your armpit while digging your wrist bone into his Achilles tendon. When done right, this lock will throw your opponent off balance and cause him a decent amount of pain. It can also cause serious damage to his ankle and knee when done with enough pressure. With your opponent stuck on one leg, you now have several options. You could push or pull on his leg, throwing him farther off balance so you can land an elbow, punch, or throw. You can kick out his grounded leg to drop him to his back. You can even run with his leg, forcing him to hop along until you find an opening. Whatever you do, it is important to unleash your attack quickly and keep your free hand guarding your face against punches. You don't want to give your opponent an opening or time to squirm his way out of the hold.

Redirecting your opponent's kick is a technique best used when you don't have a firm hold. Sometimes the kick will start to slip before you have it locked up in your armpit, in which case you can toss it in the direction it was originally heading. If you give it a good toss, usually the momentum will force your opponent to spin around in a full circle, exposing his back and giving you an opening to attack.

If the tables are turned and you happen to find your leg trapped underneath your opponent's armpit, you should attempt to maneuver out of the hold by reaching forward, grabbing your opponent's head, and then forcing his head down into the lock so you can break the hold. If your opponent doesn't have a secure lock, sometimes you can escape by turning your knee toward the ground and pulling your leg out, turning your knee up and applying downward pressure, or planting your captured foot against your opponent's chest and then forcefully pushing him back.

Catch Rear Thai Kick to Throw to Rear Thai Kick

Chun (left) is in a proper Muay Thai stance, searching for an opening on his brother.

Somphong throws a right Thai kick at Chun's midsection. Chun quickly reacts by sliding back and to his right to avoid taking the full impact, and then he catches the kick under his left arm, wrapping his hand underneath his brother's shin for a better hold. As he does this, he makes sure to keep his right hand up near his face for defense.

Twisting his hips in a clockwise direction, Chun throws Somphong's captured leg to his right. The momentum forces his brother's body to spin with his leg, exposing his back.

Before Somphong can return to his normal fighting stance, Chun takes advantage of the opening by throwing a right Thai kick to his brother's ribs.

Catch-and-Lock Rear Thai Kick to Kick-and-Sweep

Chun is in a proper Muay Thai stance, searching for an opening on his brother.

Somphong throws a right Thai kick at Chun's midsection. Chun quickly reacts by sliding back and to his right to avoid taking the full impact, and then he catches the kick under his left arm, wrapping his hand underneath his brother's shin for a better hold.

Chun secures the lock by wrapping his left arm tighter around Somphong's ankle, pinning it underneath his armpit. He then lifts up and squeezes his arm tight, driving his left wrist bone into his brother's Achilles tendon. Having control of Somphong's leg, Chun is now in a position to attack. It is important that he does this quickly because Somphong will do everything in his power to free his leg. It is also important that Chun keeps his right arm up to shield his face from possible punches.

Chun chooses a sweep for his attack. He steps in with a left low kick to Somphong's left leg, while at the same time twisting his hips and turning his upper body in the direction of the kick, cranking on his brother's leg in the process. Pulling on Somphong's leg at the moment of impact helps take weight off Somphong's grounded leg, which allows the kick to knock him off his feet. During the entire attack, Chun keeps his right hand up to guard against punches.

Catch-and-Lock Rear Thai Kick to Downward Elbow

Chun has caught Somphong's right Thai kick. To secure the hold, he wraps his left arm around Somphong's ankle, pinning it underneath his armpit. He then lifts up and squeezes his arm tight, driving his left wrist bone into his brother's Achilles tendon. Having control of Somphong's leg, Chun is now in a position to attack. It is important that he does this quickly because Somphong will do everything in his power to free his leg. It is also important that Chun keeps his right arm up to shield his face from possible punches.

Keeping his left arm tightly locked around Somphong's leg, Chun raises his right elbow. Turning his hips in a counterclockwise direction and dropping his weight into the attack, Chun drives the point of his right elbow into the side of Somphong's right thigh.

Catch-and-Lock Rear Thai Kick to Straight Knee

Chun has caught Somphong's right Thai kick. To secure the hold, he wraps his left arm around Somphong's ankle, pinning it underneath his armpit. He then lifts up and squeezes his arm tight, driving his left wrist bone into his brother's Achilles tendon. Having control of Somphong's leg, Chun is now in a position to attack. It is important that he does this quickly because Somphong will do everything in his power to free his leg. It is also important that Chun keeps his right arm up to shield his face from possible punches.

Keeping his left arm tightly locked around Somphong's leg, Chun takes a step forward and grabs the back of Somphong's head with his right hand. Pulling his brother's head down into the attack, Chun drives his right knee into Somphong's stomach.

Catch-and-Lock Rear Thai Kick to Right Cross

Chun has caught Somphong's right Thai kick. To secure the hold, he wraps his left arm around Somphong's ankle, pinning it underneath his armpit. He then lifts up and squeezes his arm tight, driving his left wrist bone into his brother's Achilles tendon. Having control of Somphong's leg, Chun is now in a position to attack. It is important that he does this quickly because Somphong will do everything in his power to free his leg. It is also important that Chun keeps his right arm up to shield his face from possible punches.

Keeping a tight lock on Somphong's right leg, Chun steps in, turns his hips in a counterclockwise direction, and throws a cross into Somphong's jaw.

COUNTER REAR THAI KICK WITH SIDE KICK

The best time to use this counter is when your opponent is telegraphing his Thai kicks. If landed clean, it will send your opponent down to the ground, and in extreme circumstances, break his leg. However, it requires good timing and pinpoint accuracy, making it very difficult to pull off. If you miss your counter kick or land it at the wrong time, you will most likely take a clean kick to the back of your head.

Chun is in a proper Muay Thai stance, searching for an opening on his brother.

Somphong throws a right Thai kick at Chun. Reacting to the attack, Chun counters with a left side kick to Somphong's grounded leg. Because Chun's attack is linear and Somphong's attack is circular, Chun's kick lands first. He makes contact with the inside of Somphong's left knee and sends him to the mat.

Countering Punches

PARRYING

Parrying is a basic counter that involves moving your hand in the way of the attack and then deflecting it to the side. Which hand you use to parry depends upon how your opponent is standing and what punch he throws. For example, if you and your opponent are both squared up in standard fighting stances and he throws a jab, you will want to parry it with your right hand. If your opponent throws a jab from within a southpaw stance, then you will parry with your left hand. Your parrying hand will always be the opposite hand to the one your opponent is using to punch.

It is important to note that the parry is not a dramatic movement. You don't want to get into the habit of reaching out with the parry because your opponent will pick up on it. He'll throw a fake jab to get you to expose your face, and then follow up with another punch. Because of this, your hand should hardly move from its position in your stance, just far enough to fall on the punch and redirect it. And to make the most of the parry, you should always throw a counterpunch either immediately after the parry or at the same time. For example, if you parry a jab with your left hand, at the same time you throw a cross with your right hand. The parry allows your opponent's momentum to continue forward, throwing him off balance, and then your right cross meets his forward momentum.

Parry Jab to Cross

Chun is in a proper Muay Thai stance, searching for an opening on his brother.

Somphong throws a cross at Chun's chin. Reacting to the attack, Chun brings his left hand down onto the punch and deflects it to the side. Before Somphong has a chance to bring his jab hand back up to guard his face, Chun retaliates with a cross.

HAND SWEEPS

A hand sweep is basically a more dramatic parry. Instead of merely redirecting your opponent's punch, you're going to parry and then sweep your opponent's punching hand out of the way. This will make your opponent vulnerable on one side, allowing you to punch with the same hand you just executed the sweep with. The maneuver is best applied against opponents who are slow to retract their hands after punching. It is important to note, however, that this move is just like the parry in that it doesn't require dramatic movement on your part. The idea is to redirect your opponent's punch just enough to create an opening for a counter.

Hand Sweep Jab to Cross

Chun is in a proper Muay Thai stance, searching for an opening on his brother.

Somphong throws a jab at Chun's chin. Reacting to the punch, Chun parries the punch by bringing his right hand down on top of Somphong's fist. Chun then redirects the punch by swinging his right arm down, tossing Somphong's left arm to the outside of his body. In the split second that the left side of Somphong's face is left unguarded, Chun throws a right cross to his jaw. It is important to note that Chun doesn't bring his right hand back into its proper place in his stance before throwing the cross. Instead, he throws the right cross immediately after the hand sweep. The punch doesn't pack as much power, but it is a sneaky blow that has a good possibility of landing.

BOBBING AND WEAVING VERSUS SIDESTEPPING

In Western boxing, bobbing and weaving work wonderfully. A good boxer will bend and lean at the hips to avoid punches and set up punches of his own. It is a good skill to possess, but it doesn't translate well to Muay Thai. If your opponent sees you bobbing and weaving, he will most likely cause you to bob or weave by throwing a fake, and then blast a kick or knee to whichever side you are leaning to. He might also throw a low kick because it will be very hard for you to check a kick while in this compromising position. For these reasons, Thai boxers rarely bob and weave. They avoid punches by parrying, side-stepping, or pivoting.

Step Out to Cross

Chun is in a proper Muay Thai stance, searching for an opening on his brother.

Somphong throws a right cross at Chun's jaw. Reacting to the attack, Chun takes a small step to his left with his lead foot, and then pivots on the ball of his left foot in a counterclockwise direction. At the same time, he uses his left hand to guide his brother's punch on its original course, carrying Somphong's weight forward. Forcefully throwing Somphong's right arm to the ground with his left hand, Chun steps in and throws a right cross.

Clinch Counters

Landing a counter from in the clinch requires tremendous sensitivity. When tied up, it only takes a second for your opponent to throw a knee at your midsection, and in that split second you have to be able to feel his movement and react, throwing him to the side he left weak by raising his leg. While doing this, however, you have to be watchful of your opponent countering your counter. For example, if you attempt a throw when your opponent executes a side knee, but you are not quick with your movements, then your opponent might use your unbalanced state to throw you in the same direction you were trying to throw him. Your goal will then be to regain your balance and throw your opponent before he can regain his balance.

Because it is such a back-and-forth battle in the clinch, each fighter waiting for his opponent to make a move so he can counter, faking is often heavily employed. An example would be leaning back to get your opponent to follow and then quickly stepping out to the side. Your opponent will continue in the original direction, leaving you in a perfect spot to throw an attack. There are counters against knees and elbows. There are counters to get out of holds and for throws. Many of these techniques are shown in this section, but the only way to make sense of them is to put as many hours as you can into clinch sparring. It is through sparring that you will develop sensitivity to your opponent's movements, and sensitivity will be your greatest weapon in the clinch.

Countering Uppercut Elbow to Elbow

Chun is in the clinching range with his brother.

Somphong throws a left uppercut elbow at Chun's chin. Reacting to the attack, Chun leans back and allows Somphong's elbow to pass. Before Somphong can return to his fighting stance, Chun steps in and throws a right side elbow to his brother's jaw.

Counter Side Knee with Under-Hook Throw

Chun is tied up in the clinch with his brother.

Somphong lifts his left leg to throw a side knee at Chun's ribs. Reacting to the attack, Chun reaches under Somphong's left leg with his right hand, securing an under-hook. Pulling down on the back of Somphong's head with his left hand and lifting up Somphong's left leg with his right arm, Chun turns his body in a counterclockwise direction and throws Somphong to the ground.

Counter Side Knee with Push Out

Chun is tied up in the clinch with his brother.

Somphong lifts his left leg to throw a side knee at Chun's ribs.

Sensing the attack, Chun takes a small step to his right side and pivots in a counterclockwise direction on his right foot. At the same time, he pushes on Somphong's head with his right arm and pulls on Somphong's right arm with his left hand. Turning his entire body in a counterclockwise direction, Chun throws Somphong to the mat.

Counter Side Knee with Pull

Chun is tied up in the clinch with his brother.

Somphong brings his left leg up to throw a side knee at Chun's ribs.

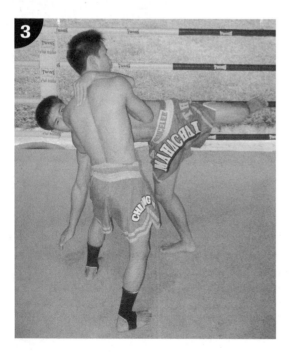

Sensing the attack, Chun turns his body in a counterclockwise direction, pulling his brother's head in the same direction with his left hand. At the same time, he pushes against his brother's ribs with his right hand. The combined movement throws Somphong off balance, and he topples to the mat.

PAD WORK AND COMBINATIONS

Basics of Pad Work and Combinations

The best way to be offensive and take charge of a fight is to put your attacks together in combinations. An array of combinations should be practiced on the Thai pads and focus mitts because this is where you will learn how to break down the movements required to string your attacks together. Certain techniques flow more fluidly into other techniques, such as a jab to a cross or a jab to a rear leg Thai kick. It will take time to learn what techniques will create an opening on your opponent and then what techniques can capitalize on that opening. It takes time to know what to throw, when to throw it, and where to target it. But if you put in that time, you will immediately spot openings and instinctively use the weapon best designed to hit your target, which may create another opening and add another attack to your combination.

Rhythm is also important, especially when you are on the receiving end of a combination. Each attack thrown can be counted as a beat. If you are operating on the same beat as your opponent, the best you can hope for is to block or check all the attacks he launches. If you can throw your own attack in between his beats, however, then you will not only disrupt his rhythm and end his combination, but also catch him out of his proper stance and land an attack. The best weapons to achieve this are the jab and front kick because they can be thrown quickly and head straight into your opponent. Your opponent will try to do the same when you are throwing a combination, so you should always be aware of what counters he can throw and react accordingly.

Learn as many of the profiled combos as you can, but by no means stick to them as if they were law. Once you get the hang of stringing your attacks together, experiment and see what works best for you. Some fighters like to follow a jab with a rear Thai kick, and some like to follow a jab with a lead leg Thai

Chun (left) is equipped with focus mitts and kicking shield, while Somphong is equipped with the Thai pads, belly pad, and shin guards.

kick. It all depends on personal preference. You will learn what works best when you apply your combinations while sparring, which should be done as much as possible, because what works on the Thai pads will not always work on an opponent.

HOLDING THE PADS

Holding the focus mitts or Thai pads is an art form in itself, and only instructors or students who have been properly taught should do it. If the pad holder calls for a certain combination and then fails to meet one of the strikes, he not only runs the risk of getting hit with the blow, but also injuring the person executing the attack. Being a pad holder requires that you exert the correct amount of pressure when a strike lands. If you apply too little pressure for a punch, the attacker could hyperextend his arm. If you apply too much pressure for a punch, the attacker could fold his wrist. The angle at which you hold the pads is also important. The idea is to hold the pads at the same angle the strike is coming in. If the attacker is throwing a straight punch, you will need to hold the pad so it meets the punch straight on. If your opponent throws an uppercut, you will have to angle the pad down to meet the punch. For kicks, it is imperative that you hold the pads so the attacker can hit them with his shin, or he might hyperextend his foot. The goal is to make the pads as much like a human as possible, meaning the same angles and resistance.

Focus Mitts

Drilling with the focus mitts is a great way to develop your boxing skills. This is where you will learn how to punch and elbow at the proper angles, and then how to put those strikes together into solid combinations. Punching the heavy bag is always good, but on the focus mitts you will get accustomed to striking at a moving target. Training with the focus mitts at least a couple of times a week will improve your speed, judgment of distance, and timing.

HOW TO HOLD THE MITTS

The Jab

The Cross

The Hook

The Uppercut

The Body Hook

FOCUS MITT COMBINATIONS

Jab to Cross to Hook

PAD HOLDER: Somphong holds out the mitt on his left hand so Chun can throw a jab. As the strike comes in, Somphong provides slight resistance to mimic an opponent's face. It is important that he doesn't provide too much resistance, because then Chun could roll or break his wrist. It is equally as important that he doesn't provide too little resistance, or Chun could hyperextend his arm.

ATTACKER: Chun throws a left jab.

PAD HOLDER: Somphong brings forward the focus mitt on his right hand immediately after the jab so Chun can see his next target. He then catches the cross with the center of the pad. It is important that he doesn't provide too much resistance, because then Chun could roll or break his wrist. It is equally as important that he doesn't provide too little resistance, because then Chun could hyperextend his arm.

ATTACKER: Seeing the right focus mitt go up, Chun knows he needs to follow the jab with the right cross. He develops power for the cross by using the backward momentum of the jab to help spring his right fist forward, throwing his left shoulder back, and snapping his hips in a counterclockwise direction.

PAD HOLDER: As the cross lands, Somphong immediately holds out the focus mitt on his left hand so Chun can see his next target. Instead of pointing the surface of the pad at Chun, he positions it at a ninety-degree angle to catch the hook.

ATTACKER: Chun sees the left focus mitt go up and knows he needs to throw a hook. To develop power for the punch, he throws his right shoulder back and rotates his hips in a clockwise direction.

Uppercut to Hook to Cross

PAD HOLDER: Somphong informs Chun that he wants a right uppercut by holding out his right hand and angling the surface of the pad toward the ground.

ATTACKER: Chun starts the combination by throwing an uppercut with his right hand.

PAD HOLDER: Just as the uppercut lands, Somphong brings his left hand up and out to show Chun that he wants a left hook next.

ATTACKER: While drawing his right hand back to his face for protection, Chun develops power for the hook by pulling his right shoulder back and whipping his hips in a clockwise direction.

PAD HOLDER: When the hook impacts, Somphong holds up his right hand to show Chun the next punch in the combination will be a cross.

ATTACKER: While drawing his left hand back toward his face, Chun develops power for the right cross by pulling his left shoulder back and spinning his hips in a counterclockwise direction.

Jab to Cross to Step Out to Cross

PAD HOLDER: Somphong holds up his left hand to show Chun that he wants a jab. **ATTACKER:** Chun throws a left jab.

PAD HOLDER: Somphong brings forward the focus mitt on his right hand immediately after the jab so Chun can see his next target. He then catches the cross with the center of the pad. **ATTACKER:** Seeing the right focus mitt go up, Chun knows he needs to follow the jab with the right cross. He develops power for the cross by using the backward momentum of the jab to help spring his right fist forward, throwing his left shoulder back, and snapping his hips in a counterclockwise direction.

PAD HOLDER: Somphong tests Chun's awareness by throwing a left jab at his face. He makes sure not to throw too hard because the edge of he focus mitt could easily break Chun's nose. **ATTACKER:** Chun reacts to the attack by sliding to his right and turning his body in a counterclockwise direction. At the same time, he checks Somphong's jab with his left hand.

PAD HOLDER: Somphong turns his body toward Chun and puts up his right hand to show the next punch in the combination will be a cross.
ATTACKER: Chun throws a right cross.

Jab to Hook to Cross

PAD HOLDER: Somphong holds up his left hand to show Chun that he wants a jab.
ATTACKER: Chun throws a left jab.

PAD HOLDER: When the jab makes impact, Somphong holds up his left hand to show Chun that he wants a hook to follow.

ATTACKER: Seeing that Somphong wants a left hook, Chun brings his left hand halfway back to his face and then whips his left shoulder and hips in a clockwise direction. Rotating on the ball of his left foot, he brings his left elbow up so it is level with the target. Staying relaxed, he snaps a left hook into the pad.

PAD HOLDER: Just after the hook lands, Somphong drops his left hand and brings up his right to show Chun that he wants a cross.

ATTACKER: Seeing the right focus mitt go up, Chun knows he needs to follow the hook with the right cross. He develops power for the cross by using the backward momentum of the hook to help spring his right fist forward, throwing his left shoulder back, and snapping his hips in a counterclockwise direction.

Body-Cross to Uppercut to Elbow

PAD HOLDER: Somphong calls out a body blow and then holds both hands up to show Chun that he wants him to strike the belly pad.
ATTACKER: Chun drops his weight down to execute a cross to the body.

PAD HOLDER: As the cross lands, Somphong holds out his left hand, angling the surface of the pad toward the ground to show Chun he wants an uppercut.
ATTACKER: Chun follows the cross with an uppercut, rotating his hips in a clockwise direction and driving up off his front foot to get power for the punch.

PAD HOLDER: Somphong brings his right hand forward into clinching range, showing Chun that he wants a right side elbow.
ATTACKER: Taking a small step with his lead leg, Chun turns his hips in a counterclockwise direction and snaps a right side elbow into the target.

Jab to Block to Uppercut Elbow to Side Elbow

PAD HOLDER: Somphong holds up his left hand to show Chun he wants a jab.
ATTACKER: Chun throws a left jab.

PAD HOLDER: Somphong checks Chun's reactions by throwing a left hook at his head, trying to hit Chun with the flat surface of the mitt.
ATTACKER: Reacting to the attack, Chun presses his right arm tightly against the side of his face, blocking the hook with his arm and shoulder.

PAD HOLDER: Somphong brings his right hand forward into clinching range and angles the pad slightly down. This shows Chun that he wants a right uppercut elbow.
ATTACKER: Seeing the next technique in the combination, Chun delivers a right uppercut elbow immediately after the block.

PAD HOLDER: Somphong keeps his right hand out and angles the pad ninety degrees to his left to show Chun that he wants a right side elbow.

ATTACKER: Immediately after the uppercut elbow, Chun drops his right elbow down slightly and then loops it around in a small circle, executing a right side elbow.

Jab to Counter Jab to Overhand Right to Hook

PAD HOLDER: Somphong puts out his left hand to indicate that he wants a jab.

ATTACKER: Chun throws a left jab.

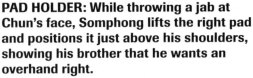

PAD HOLDER: While throwing a jab at Chun's face, Somphong lifts the right pad and positions it just above his shoulders, showing his brother that he wants an overhand right.

ATTACKER: Chun reacts by throwing the overhand right. In doing so, he tilts his body slightly to his left side to get the appropriate downward angle for the punch, allowing him to slip his brother's jab.

PAD HOLDER: Somphong pulls his left hand halfway back and turns it to the side, indicating that he wants a left hook.

ATTACKER: Chun takes a step back with his right leg and turns his hips and left shoulder in a clockwise direction, snapping his hook into the target.

Jab to Check to Cross

PAD HOLDER: Somphong puts out his left hand to indicate that he wants a jab.
ATTACKER: Chun throws a left jab.

PAD HOLDER: Somphong tests Chun's reactions by firing a left Thai kick at his brother's rear leg.
ATTACKER: Reacting to the attack, Chun checks the kick with his rear leg.

PAD HOLDER: As Somphong drops his kicking leg, he brings his right hand up to indicate that he wants a right cross. It is important that he does this immediately after the kick so Chun can see his next target and set up his shot.
ATTACKER: Seeing that his brother wants a right cross, Chun turns his left shoulder and hips in a counterclockwise direction as he shoots his right leg back to the ground, adding power to the cross.

Thai Pads

Training on the Thai pads allows you to work on striking in all the ranges of combat. In a matter of seconds, you can transition from kicking range to punching range to clinching range, or the other way around. It helps you put all your tools together and gives you a sense of what it is like to strike a person. At first it is beneficial to have the instructor or whoever is holding the pads call out which strike he wants just before holding up the pad. When you see your target, unleash with the strike without hesitating. Pretty soon, you will no longer have to be told which strike to throw. The moment you see a pad go up, you'll lash out with the proper technique. After developing some rapport with the pad holder, eventually you will be able to throw your own attacks, and he will be able to react by putting the pads in the proper place to catch them. This should not be attempted, however, if the pad holder is uncertain about how to hold the pads.

As with all drills, you should focus on your technique when working the Thai pads, but you should also push yourself to increase your endurance. If you're planning on fighting, you should be able to throw a nonstop barrage of punches, kicks, elbows, and knees for five three-minute rounds on the Thai pads without getting overly winded. If you're like most Thai boxers, Thai pads will be the bread and butter of your training.

HOLDING THE THAI PADS

Jab

Cross

Push Kick

Right Thai Kick

Left Thai Kick

Right Knee

Left Knee

THAI PAD COMBINATIONS

Jab to Thai Kick

PAD HOLDER: Chun holds up his left arm to show Somphong that he wants a jab.
ATTACKER: Somphong hits the middle of the Thai pad with a jab.

PAD HOLDER: Pivoting in a counter-clockwise direction on his left foot, Chun presses his elbows together so that the Thai pads form a solid barrier on his left side. This tells his brother that he wants a right Thai kick to the midsection.
ATTACKER: To generate power for the kick, Somphong pulls his left shoulder back as he retracts the jab and turns his hips in a counterclockwise direction.

Cross to Thai Kick

PAD HOLDER: Chun holds up his right arm to show his brother that he wants a cross.
ATTACKER: Somphong throws a cross to the center of the Thai pad.

PAD HOLDER: Turning his hips slightly in a clockwise direction, Chun presses his elbows together so that the Thai pads form a solid barrier on his right side. This informs his brother that he wants a left leg Thai kick.
ATTACKER: Immediately following the cross, Somphong steps forward with his right foot, covering the distance needed to throw a left Thai kick to the midsection.

PAD HOLDER: Chun provides resistance as the kick connects with the pads.
ATTACKER: Somphong unleashes a left Thai kick.

Jab to Push Kick to Knee

PAD HOLDER: Chun holds up his left arm to show his brother that he wants a jab as the first strike in the combination.
ATTACKER: Somphong throws a jab to the middle of the Thai pad.

PAD HOLDER: Chun drops both pads down to this side, which indicates to his brother that he wants a front kick to the belly pad as the next strike.
ATTACKER: Somphong throws a push kick with his leg to the center of the belly pad.

PAD HOLDER: Chun places his right arm across the top of the belly pad, indicating to his brother that he should throw a right knee.
ATTACKER: As Somphong drops his left foot to the ground, he grabs Chun's head with his right hand in preparation for the knee. It is important to notice that he is guarding his face with his left arm.

PAD HOLDER: Staying balanced, Chun stops any upward progression of the knee by pressing down with his right arm upon impact.
ATTACKER: Pulling on Chun's head, Somphong drives his knee into the belly pad.

Jab to Cross to Counter Push Kick to Thai Kick

PAD HOLDER: Chun holds up his left arm to indicate to Somphong that he wants a jab. **ATTACKER:** Somphong throws a left jab at the middle of the Thai pad.

PAD HOLDER: As Somphong's jab lands, Chun immediately holds up his right arm to show the next strike will be a cross. **ATTACKER:** Pulling his left shoulder back to help rotate his hips in a counterclockwise direction, Somphong throws a right cross at the center of the Thai pad.

PAD HOLDER: As Somphong returns to his fighting stance after the cross, Chun checks his brother's reactions by throwing a left push kick. **ATTACKER:** Reacting to the attack, Somphong steps back with his left leg, putting him in a right lead stance (southpaw). At the same time, he catches the kick with his right hand.

ATTACKER: Somphong tosses Chun's leg to the side using his right hand and then immediately steps in for a left Thai kick.
PAD HOLDER: As Chun falls to his right side, he immediately presses his elbows together, forming a solid barrier with the Thai pads so he can catch his brother's kick.

Hook to Thai Kick to Check to Knee

PAD HOLDER: Chun holds out his left arm at a forty-five degree angle so that his brother needs to reposition his body in order to land a left hook.
ATTACKER: Somphong pivots in a clockwise direction on his left foot, giving him a new angle of attack for the left hook.

PAD HOLDER: Chun pivots in a counterclockwise direction on his right foot and pinches his elbows together, forming a solid barrier with the Thai pads on his left side to catch his brother's kick.
ATTACKER: Immediately following the hook, Somphong throws a right Thai kick.

PAD HOLDER: Immediately after Somphong returns to his fighting stance, Chun throws a Thai kick with his left leg.
ATTACKER: Stepping back into his stance, Somphong raises his right leg to check his brother's left Thai kick.

PAD HOLDER: Bringing his leg straight down from his kick, Chun leans forward and places the right Thai pad across the top of the belly pad to indicate he wants the next strike to be a knee. He holds out the left Thai pad to ensure Somphong doesn't lean into the knee.

ATTACKER: Instead of dropping his right leg back into his normal stance after checking the kick, Somphong steps his right foot forward, putting him into a southpaw stance. This allows him to cover the distance needed to grab the back of his brother's head and drive a straight knee into the belly pad.

Low Thai Kick to Thai Kick to Elbow to Push-and-Step Out to Knee

PAD HOLDER: Chun calls out an inside leg kick, and then he holds his ground so his brother can execute the technique.

ATTACKER: Somphong throws the kick to the inside of his brother's leg, using only light power so as not to hurt him.

ATTACKER: Instead of dropping his left leg down into its lead position, Somphong uses the force of the kick to push his left leg to the rear, putting him in a southpaw stance. With his left leg now in the power position, he fires a left Thai kick into the pads.

PAD HOLDER: Chun allows Somphong to pull his left arm down, and then he turns his body in a counterclockwise direction so he can catch his brother's right side elbow with the pad on his right arm.

ATTACKER: Turning his hips in a counterclockwise direction, Somphong traps Chun's left arm to clear an opening for his right side elbow.

PAD HOLDER: Standing his ground and allowing his brother to pivot around him, Chun drops the right pad down and lays it across the top of the belly pad. Upon impact, he presses his right arm down to stop the upward momentum of the knee strike.

ATTACKER: After landing the elbow strike, Somphong pivots in a clockwise direction on his left foot. At the same time, he brings his left arm up and wraps his hand around the back of his brother's head. Applying downward pressure with his left hand, he brings his right hand over and places it above his left. Pulling down with both hands to throw off his brother's balance, he fires a straight knee into Chun's midsection.

Knee to Elbow to Push to Thai Kick

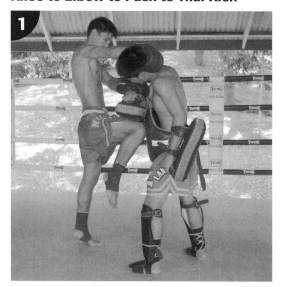

PAD HOLDER: Chun places the right Thai pad across the top of the belly pad, indicating that the first technique in the combination should be a right straight knee.

ATTACKER: Somphong steps in, places his right hand on the back of his brother's head, traps his brother's right arm with his left hand, and then pulls Chun's head down as he drives in a straight knee.

PAD HOLDER: Immediately after the knee, Chun holds out the left Thai pad at a forty-five degree angle to his brother. Because they are in clinching range, it is an indication that he wants a left side elbow.
ATTACKER: As Somphong drops his left foot back to return to his normal fighting stance, he rotates his hips in a clockwise direction to add power to his left side elbow attack.

PAD HOLDER: Immediately after Somphong lands the elbow strike, Chun throws a left Thai kick at his brother's midsection.
ATTACKER: Countering the attack, Somphong straightens out his left arm and pushes on his brother's chest, knocking Chun back.

PAD HOLDER: Using the momentum of the push, Chun drops his left leg back and throws up the Thai pads on his left side, indicating to his brother that he wants a right Thai kick.

ATTACKER: Somphong immediately throws a right Thai kick.

Step Out to Knee

PAD HOLDER: Chun advances on his brother by stepping forward.

ATTACKER: Somphong steps forward with his right foot and pivots his hips in a counterclockwise direction. He drops his right hand down on top of Chun's left wrist to help guide his brother's momentum past him.

PAD HOLDER: Chun pivots in a counterclockwise direction on the ball of his left foot to set his brother up for the attack. By dropping his right arm and laying it across the top of the belly pad, he indicates to Somphong that he wants a left straight knee.

ATTACKER: Rotating in a clockwise direction on the ball of his right foot, Somphong grabs the back of Chun's head with his left hand. At the same time, he maintains his grip on Chun's left arm with his right hand, using both of his hands to pull his brother down into his straight knee.

Jab to Cross to Check to Step to Knee

PAD HOLDER: Chun holds up his left arm for a jab.
ATTACKER: Somphong throws a jab to the center of the Thai pad.

PAD HOLDER: As the jab makes contact with his left arm, Chun holds up his right arm for the cross.
ATTACKER: Pulling his left shoulder back as he retracts his jab, Somphong rotates his hips in a counterclockwise direction and throws a cross at the center of the Thai pad.

PAD HOLDER: Immediately after Somphong's cross, Chun throws a Thai kick with his right leg to ensure his brother isn't getting too stretched out on his punches.
ATTACKER: Retracting his cross, Somphong brings up his left leg to check the Thai kick.

PAD HOLDER: After retracting his kick, Chun drops his weight and places his right arm across the belly pad to indicate that he wants a right straight knee next.

ATTACKER: Instead of dropping his left leg back to its position in his stance, Somphong steps forward off the check and reaches his right hand to the back of Chun's head so he can pull him into his knee attack. He traps Chun's right arm with his left hand to avoid any counterpunches.

Check to Step to Knee to Clinch to Turn to Knee

PAD HOLDER: To start off the combination, Chun throws a Thai kick with his left leg.
ATTACKER: Somphong throws up a right check to block Chun's Thai kick.

PAD HOLDER: After throwing the Thai kick, Chun drops his leg and places his right arm across the top of the belly pad to indicate to his brother that he wants a left straight knee next. He puts his left arm straight out to ensure Somphong doesn't lean forward into the attack.

ATTACKER: Instead of bringing his checking leg back into his normal stance, Somphong drops his right foot to the front, putting him in a southpaw stance. He traps Chun's left arm with his right hand to avoid counterpunches and grabs the back of his brother's head with his left hand to pull him into the knee.

PAD HOLDER: After Somphong lands the straight knee, Chun ties him up in the clinch.

ATTACKER: Somphong drops his left foot after landing the knee. He works his arms to the inside of his brother's arms and wraps his hands around his head, securing a dominant clinch position.

ATTACKER: Somphong steps to the outside of Chun's left leg with his right foot. He then pivots in a counterclockwise direction on his right foot, using his left hand to pull Chun around into his attack. **PAD HOLDER:** Chun maintains balance as he follows Somphong's movement, preparing for the straight knee by dropping his right arm and laying it across the top of the belly pad.

PAD HOLDER: Chun presses his right arm down into the attack to keep the knee from slipping up and striking his sternum. He extends his left hand to ensure Somphong doesn't lean forward into the strike. **ATTACKER:** Somphong pulls down on Chun's head with both hands as he drives in his left knee.

DRILLS, CONDITIONING, AND STRENGTH TRAINING

Drills

HEAVY BAG

Training on the heavy bag will be one of your primary ways to develop power, speed, and a good sense of timing and distance. To make the most of your heavy bag training, you should treat it as if it were an opponent standing directly in front of you. Forgetting to keep your hands up or throwing your techniques without power will only cause you to acquire bad habits. An all-too-common sight in Thai boxing gyms is a student just aimlessly pounding away on the heavy bag with no real goal in mind. Although this might increase your conditioning and fitness, it won't make you any better at Muay Thai techniques. You should perform all your techniques as if you were using them in a fight, which means that you should concentrate on speed, power, balance, timing, and your distance from your imaginary opponent. A lot of students also make the mistake of being stationary or fully offensive when freestyle training on the heavy bag. It's important that you're always moving, using good footwork and stepping in and out of range to set up techniques. Pretend the sway of the bag is your opponent's movements, and then react to those movements with both counters and defense. Stepping out of the way or stopping the bag's sway with a counterattack such as a push kick or round kick can achieve this. Also, throw up blocks and checks and fakes here and there to keep each round on the heavy bag like a simulated fight. If you train in this manner all the time, it will make you a better fighter and better prepare you to step into the ring.

Although freestyle training on the heavy bag is extremely beneficial, you will also want to do rounds where you focus on specific techniques or combinations. One round you could focus exclusively on your hand techniques, and then the following round use your punches to set up your other weapons, such as a knee or kick off a three-punch combination. This exercise is an excellent way to learn how to put all your tools together.

The heavy bag is also a good way to toughen up your body for an upcoming fight. The constant pounding will condition your shins, knees, hands, and elbows for combat. This will take time, and you should expect soreness and tenderness in the beginning. But as the weeks go by, you will notice your body growing accustomed to the impact. It is important, however, that you use the proper gear when training with the heavy bag. With heavy bags being unforgiving, you should always wear hand wraps to avoid folding your wrist or damaging your knuckles. The persistent pounding can also take a toll on your joints, so listen to your body. If your legs are sore or injured, focus on isolating your hands. If your knuckles are sore, focus on knees and kicks. This is good training because you might encounter a similar situation in the ring and need to isolate techniques to make it to the end of the bout. But if your entire body is beat up, focus on something else. There are many other nonimpact drills and exercises you can do if your body needs a few days' rest to recover.

Jumping Knees. In Thailand, most Muay Thai camps require their fighters to do between five hundred and a thousand jumping knees a day on the heavy bag. The reasons are many: they're a pivotal part of gaining endurance; they're a dangerous weapon when tied up in the clinch; they're a beautiful technique that scores highly on the judges' scorecards; they're one of the most difficult techniques to perform because you can easily be thrown off balance while your feet are off the ground. Fighters who can execute this technique time and again during a fight are crowd-pleasers, and every fighter should aim for this goal, because what pleases the crowd usually pleases the judges. The best way to get good at jumping knees is by doing thousands of repetitions on the heavy bag. The optimum time to execute these drills is at the end of your training session when you are tired. They will force you to give that one last push to further develop your conditioning. Most do fifty at a time with a thirty-second or one-minute break between sets.

To drill jumping straight knees, start by wrapping both hands around the sides of the heavy bag near the top. You should grip the bag as if it were an opponent's head because your hold will control the movement of the bag. Then get into a proper clinch stance: body slightly square, balanced on the balls of your feet, hips slightly out, and your chin hidden by your shoulders. To throw a jumping straight knee with your right leg, step your left foot toward your right foot, and then immediately swing your right leg straight back. When done correctly, your left foot will land in almost the exact same spot that your right foot just left. As your right leg reaches the end of its backward path, use your arms to pull yourself into the bag and spring off your left foot. Then drive your right knee into the bag by thrusting your hips forward. After the strike has landed, come down onto your left foot and repeat with the opposite leg.

Push Kicks on the Heavy Bag. Push kicks are another technique that can be isolated on the heavy bag for the purpose of developing speed, power, balance, timing, and a sense of distance. A good drill is to execute a hundred consecutive push kicks with each leg, hitting the same spot on the bag time and again. You can throw your kicks from your fighting stance, while balancing on one leg, or by setting them up with a skip step. Whichever technique you employ, you want to acquire a rhythm with the bag by kicking it away and then waiting for it to swing back at you before kicking it again.

Trading Push Kicks on the Heavy Bag. Once you acquire the timing, rhythm, and distance needed to land repeated push kicks on the heavy bag, it can be fun and beneficial to switch things up by adding another person into the equation. In this drill, you and your training partner will each assume a fighting stance on opposite sides of the bag and trade push kick for push kick. The goal is to keep the heavy bag at bay by kicking at the right time and distance. This can be very hard to achieve, especially if your opponent gets tricky and kicks at odd angles.

Sometimes both of you may kick at almost exactly the same time, in which case one of you will have to kick twice in a row. It can be fun because of the competition factor, and it will be beneficial because it will further increase your timing, speed, and sense of distance.

Consecutive Thai Kicks on the Heavy Bag. This drill can be done by yourself or with a partner. When doing it by yourself, your goal will be the same as when throwing push kicks into the heavy bag—you want to kick with proper form and time each kick as the bag swings back into you. When conducting this drill with a training partner, you can stand side by side, in which case one of you will be throwing a right Thai kick and one a left Thai kick, or position yourselves on opposite sides of the bag, in which case you both will be throwing either right or left Thai kicks. In both cases, you want to fire off your kicks as your opponent is retracting his kick, making the drill twice as quick as if you were doing it alone. Like the other drills on the heavy bag, this will develop your timing, speed, balance, and endurance. You and your partner should try to do four sets of twenty-five kicks with each leg.

SPEED BAG

The speed bag is mainly used to develop hand coordination, rhythm, and conditioning. It can be extremely frustrating in the beginning, but if you stick with it eventually you'll get the rhythm down and have fun. When starting off, you should only use one hand. Begin by hitting the center of the bag with the side of your hand at a forward and downward angle. The bag will move fast, so let it hit the rear of the platform, come forward and hit the front of the platform, and then hit the rear of the platform again. When it comes at you the second time, you want to hit it again. So, the bag will hit the platform three times before you send out your second punch. Once you can keep this rhythm using one hand, add your other hand into the picture and switch between them. After getting the hang of hitting it with two hands, you can then mix up the rhythm by going slowly and then fast, as well as using different punching combinations. This will develop excellent hand-eye coordination.

TOP AND BOTTOM BAG

The top and bottom bag is another piece of equipment used to develop accuracy, rhythm, timing, and distance. The bag itself is usually the size of a small soccer ball. Suspended in the air at punching height by bungee cords connected to the ceiling and floor, the bag will bounce chaotically back and forth when punched. Just like the speed bag, it can be frustrating at first, but with time it can become a lot of fun to play with. To get a hang of the movement, you should begin by striking the bag with a snappy jab. It's not like the heavy bag; instead of focusing on power, you want to focus on speed and accuracy. How hard you hit the bag will dictate how fast it will come back at you, so when first starting out, just give it a light tap. The bag will head away and then come back. The moment it enters your striking range, you want to send out another snappy jab. If you are too slow, the bag will hit your chest. If you are too fast, you will miss. Do this over and over with the jab until you can hit the bag repeatedly. Once you have developed a sense of distance and timing, you can change the rhythm of the bag by hitting it harder or softer and throwing other punches. The cross is the easiest to add at first because it is a straight punch, but eventually you'll be throwing hooks and uppercuts, which will make things a whole lot more interesting as the bag moves not only from front to back, but also side to side.

SPARRING

Sparring is the closest thing that you will find to a real fight, making it the best way to acquire a sense of timing and distance. Sparring should be about learning and having fun, not about knocking your opponent out. A mild dose of competition should be expected and helps better both combatants, but if you hurt or injure your training partners there will be no one left to train with. It can also create bad blood. You and your training partner should always step into the ring with a common goal—to make each other better. The intentions of each sparring session should be discussed ahead of time. If the goal is to go all out and simulate a true fight, both fighters should agree on this and put on the necessary gear. An instructor should also supervise the sparring session so nothing gets out of control. But most of the time your goal should be to improve your technique, which comes from focusing on your speed rather than your power. Active fighters rarely spar hard because the risk of receiving an injury is just too great. And if they are going to fight, they might as well get paid for it. If you aren't currently fighting, then sparring hard once in a while can definitely be beneficial. It allows you to break bad habits such as pulling your strikes, as well as gives you a sense of what a real fight is like.

Sparring Drills—(Boxer Versus Kickboxer). Although sparring with all your tools is best to develop your overall game, mixing things up can be beneficial. One way to do this is to restrict what you are allowed to throw. For example, you could be limited to throwing kicks while your opponent is limited to throwing punches. Such a drill can be frustrating in the beginning because you want to utilize your other tools, but you will get more out of it than you think. If you are limited to kicks, you'll learn how to counter punches using your legs. If you are limited to hand attacks, you will learn how to counter kicks using punches. It will open your mind up to different ways to launch combinations and break the bad habit of thinking only of your upper body when you punch and only of your lower body when you kick. It can also benefit you in the future if you ever step into the ring with an opponent who has superior kicks or punches. Instead of matching his techniques and losing, you'll know how to isolate another area of your game and come out on top.

Conditioning

RUNNING

Running is an essential part of Muay Thai training. Most Thai boxing camps have extensive runs twice a day. They'll do a seven-mile run in the morning for endurance and then a five-mile run in the afternoon to warm up. The benefits are numerous: it's a great way to condition your lungs, giving you the edge in the later rounds of a fight; it toughens you both mentally and physically; the impact on the ground strengthens your legs for the abuse of Thai kicks; it improves your balance and adds power to your strikes. If you ignore the running aspect of training, your legs will be the first things to get tired in a fight. The next thing to get tired will be your hands, which is why you should hold them up at eye level when you run, strengthening your shoulders so you'll be able to keep your guard up for the duration of any battle. You must also push yourself during your runs, especially later in the week when your body is tired and broken down. Your legs might burn from lactic acid buildup, and your lungs might feel as though they can't get enough air, but pushing through your exhaustion will develop the mental strength needed for combat. Most of the time it's just a matter of overcoming that voice in your head that is telling you to stop.

Many Thai boxers find running to be the most boring part of training, but because it is an integral part of Muay Thai, those wishing to fight cannot overlook it. When your runs seem to drag out forever, there are several things you can do. You can find different routes, change the speed at which you run, change the terrain on which you run, and even vary your distances. One morning run seven miles on flat terrain, and the next morning run five miles on hilly terrain. If this doesn't make things more interesting, try listening to music on a Walkman or MP3 player. It can be a great tool to help you push the pace, as well as add rhythm to your run. The important part is that you run regularly and push yourself every time. The goal is to push yourself well past your limits so that when you actually step into the ring you'll have the mental and physical stamina to blast away until the end of the fifth round.

STADIUMS

Stadiums should be added to your run rather than serve as a substitute. If you are routinely running on flat terrain, they should be done twice a week. Because no two stadiums are alike, there is no set number of how many times you should go up and down. The important part is that you push yourself hard enough that you get your heart rate up for at least twenty minutes and get a good muscle burn. Before running stadiums, however, it is good to pay attention to the state of the stairs. Wood stairs tend to be weaker in some spots, which can cause you to trip while running up and down them. Concrete or steel stairs are the best, but it is always good to do a quick walk-through of your route before starting just to make sure the stairs are sturdy enough to hold your weight without bowing downward. And just as with running, take extra care when coming down because this is when the most stress is put upon your joints.

SPRINTS

A strong Muay Thai training program will include sprints. They can be integrated into your long-distance runs by breaking into a sprint every five minutes, holding it for a minute, and then returning to your normal run, or they can be run separately. Incorporating sprints into your run is best because it will mimic the pace of a fight—the sprint resembles the heavy exchanges you will usually experience a couple of times every round, and the normal jog resembles the pace you'll keep for the rest of the rounds. Sprints done separately will be more intense and should be done on the running track or on grass because of the heavy impact they'll put on the joints in your legs. If you are getting ready for a fight, it is good to stop doing sprints about a week to two weeks before your match to allow your legs time to rest and recover. And when doing sprints, you want to adequately warm up before and after to avoid pulling a muscle or twisting an ankle.

STRENGTH-TRAINING EXERCISES

Having huge, bulky muscles will hurt your Muay Thai game rather than improve it. In Thai boxing, you generate power for your strikes from your hips and good technique. If you try to muscle your punches and kicks, they are going to be considerably slower, easier for your opponent to see coming, and have a lot less power. Being strong, however, is not a hindrance. It will help you in all aspects of your game, especially your clinch. As a result, most Thai boxers include strength-building exercises into their routine. If you choose to lift weights, it should be done with the intention of building strength and endurance rather than bulk. The best way to achieve this is by doing high repetitions instead of power lifting. Because of your already strenuous training regimen, it is best to create a three-day routine, with each day focusing on a major and minor muscle group. For example, day one you could focus on back and triceps, day two you could focus on chest and biceps, and day three you could focus on shoulders and legs. When training the major muscle groups, you usually want to do about ten to twelve sets, each set consisting of fifteen to twenty repetitions. For your minor muscle groups, you want to do between six and eight sets, with fifteen to twenty repetitions per set. If you are unsure which machines to use to isolate your various body parts, you can hire a trainer for a couple of days or pick up a book dedicated to weight training. At the end of your three-day routine, you should take two days off to recuperate.

If you don't have a weight room to work out in or you simply don't like those types of gyms, you can certainly get sufficient training on your own. You should keep the same workout, isolating a major and minor muscle group each day of your three-day routine, but instead of hefting weights you'll be doing pull-ups, push-ups, free squats, and a dozen other exercises.

And whether you're working out in the gym or on your own, you're going to want to do plenty of abdominal exercises. You should do hundreds of sit-ups, crunches, and leg raises. The sit-ups and crunches you can do on your own, but for the leg raises you will need a partner. While lying on your back, have your partner stand up by your head. Straightening your legs, throw them up toward his chest. When they reach your partner, he will forcibly throw them back down. Stopping your legs six inches from the ground, you immediately want to throw them right back at him.

Training Program

Having a training program is important for anyone who wants to keep track of his progress and better his game. Most serious Thai boxing gyms will already have a training program that the fighters are expected to adhere to. If you cannot follow this program for whatever reason, you should ask one of the trainers to help you design one that will keep you up to par. Having a firm resolution of what you have to do and when can keep you from getting lazy. It eliminates the stress of trying to decide what you should do on a given day because everything is already outlined. It gives you goals to reach every time you step into the gym. If your training program doesn't include daily and weekly goals, then you should add them to your schedule long before you step into the gym.

It also helps if your training program outlines every detail of each training session. If you plan on training twice a day, you should have the times laid out on when you will run and when you will begin kicking the bags. The distance you plan to run should be drawn in ink, as well as the time you will spend sparring, strength training, stretching, and whatever else is included in your program. You should also include the intensity at which you plan to train. Do not cut the detail short because it's the detail that will help you make it through your program. Obviously it would be very difficult to write down every single detail of a program, but you should do as much as possible. The idea is to create a program that pushes you to be better and allows you to grow. The less you lay out ahead of time, the easier it will be to slack off and call it a day.

Keeping a journal will help you with this. During training you will often come across something you need to work on. You could be standing flat-footed while in the clinch or constantly dropping your hands. When you spot such a weakness, you should immediately write it down to keep it from slipping your mind. Later that night, come up with some drills that will help improve your weakness, and then add them into your training program for the following week. If your weakness still isn't gone at the end of the following week, add those same drills to your program for the next week. This will keep you from hitting a plateau in your training because there will always be something to work on.

PRO MUAY THAI PROGRAM

Below is an example of a professional Muay Thai training program. It doesn't include specific details such as times and goals for each round because that should be done on a personal level according to what you want to achieve. Although every Thai camp has a different regimen, as well as different days for training certain techniques, if you can make it through this program day in and day out, you are certainly headed on the right path. (All rounds are either five minutes long with a one-minute break or three-minute rounds with a thirty-second break.)

MONDAY

Morning
    Warm up and stretch
    Ten-kilometer run
    Two to five rounds shadowboxing

Two to five rounds on the heavy bag or padded rounds with instructor

Three hundred jumping knees on the heavy bag

One hundred push kicks with each leg on the heavy bag

Two hundred sit-ups

Cool down and stretch

Afternoon

Warm up and stretch

Five-kilometer run and/or half an hour of skipping rope

Two to five rounds shadowboxing

Five rounds on the heavy bag

Three to five padded rounds with instructor

An hour to an hour and a half of clinch sparring, switching off with different opponents

Three hundred jumping knees or two hundred straight knees with each leg on the heavy bag

One hundred Thai kicks with each leg on the heavy bag

Strength training

Cool down and stretch

TUESDAY

Morning

Warm up and stretch

Ten-kilometer run

Two to five rounds shadowboxing

Two to five rounds on heavy bag or padded rounds with instructor

Three hundred knees or one hundred kicks each leg

Two hundred sit-ups

Cool down and stretch

Afternoon

Warm up and stretch

Five-kilometer run and/or half an hour of skipping rope

Three to five rounds shadowboxing

Three to five rounds on the heavy bag

Three to five padded rounds with instructor

Clinch sparring for half an hour to one hour

Three hundred jumping knees or one hundred push kicks each leg

Strength training

Two hundred sit-ups

Cool down and stretch

WEDNESDAY

Morning

Warm up and stretch

Seven-kilometer mountain run or a ten-kilometer run on flat terrain

Two hundred sit-ups

Cool down and stretch

Afternoon

Warm up and stretch

Five-kilometer run and/or half an hour of skipping rope

Three to five rounds shadowboxing

Three to five rounds on the heavy bag or other equipment (top and bottom bag, speed bag)

Three to five padded rounds with instructor

Clinch sparring for an hour to an hour and a half

Strength training

Two hundred sit-ups

Cool down and stretch

THURSDAY

Morning

Warm up and stretch

Seven-kilometer run (optional: one-minute sprints every five to ten minutes)

Two to five rounds shadowboxing

Three to five rounds on the heavy bag

Three hundred knees on the heavy bag

One hundred Thai kicks each leg or one hundred push kicks each
    leg

Two hundred sit-ups

Cool down and stretch

Afternoon

Warm up and stretch

Five-kilometer run and/or half an hour of skipping rope

Two to five rounds shadowboxing

Three to five rounds on the heavy bag

Three to five padded rounds with instructor

Two to five rounds sparring, utilizing only hand techniques

Clinch sparring for one hour to an hour and a half

Strength training

Two hundred sit-ups

Cool down and stretch

FRIDAY

Morning

Warm up and stretch

Ten-kilometer run

Two hundred sit-ups

Cool down and stretch

Afternoon

Warm up and stretch

Five-kilometer run or half an hour of skipping rope

Two to five rounds shadowboxing

Five rounds on the heavy bag

Five padded rounds with instructor

Clinch sparring for one hour

Strength training

Cool down and stretch

SATURDAY

Morning

    Warm up and stretch

    Forty-five-minute mountain run

    Cool down and stretch

Afternoon

    Warm up and stretch

    Half an hour of skipping rope

    Two to five rounds shadowboxing

    Five rounds on the heavy bag

    Five padded rounds with instructor

    Two to five rounds sparring using all techniques

    Clinch sparring for one hour

    Strength training

    Cool down and stretch

SUNDAY

Off

Index